Waldorf Schools

Volume II

Waldorf Schools

Volume II

Upper Grades and High School

Thirty-four articles from "Education as an Art",
Bulletin of the Waldorf Schools of North America
1940 - 1978

Selected, edited and
with an introduction
by Ruth Pusch

MERCURY PRESS
Spring Valley, New York
1993

All rights reserved.
Cover design by Maryann Perlman
Cover painting, tenth grade,
Highland Hall, Los Angeles

Copyright © 1993 by Mercury Press

ISBN 0-929979-30-3

Published in the USA by:

MERCURY PRESS
Fellowship Community
241 Hungry Hollow Road
Spring Valley, NY 10977

Contents

Introduction 1
    Ruth Pusch

I. IDEAS AND INSIGHTS

What is so Special about the Waldorf Schools? 8
    Erich Gabert
At the Beginning 11
    Herbert Hahn
Study of Man 14
    A.C. Harwood
The Community Sense in Child and Adult 19
    Marjorie Spock
Principles and Growing Human Beings 24
    Hermann Poppelbaum
Some Characteristics of Steiner Education:
A Radio Interview 29
    Henry Barnes
Of Machines and Men 36
    Ernst Katz
Independence in Education 45
    Dorothy Harrer
Linear Thinking 48
    Christoph Lindenberg
It's Easy to Start a Waldorf School, But... 53
    Shirley & Bob Routledge
Waldorf Education and the Public Schools 59
    James Peterson

II. ELEMENTARY SCHOOL, UPPER GRADES

A Class as a Community 67
    Dorothy Harrer
How to Present the Drama of Sound to Twelve-Year-Olds ... 73
    Karl Ege
The Chladni Plate 76
    Gerhard Bedding
The Education of the Will in the Crafts Lesson 79
    Wolfgang Wagner
Wish, Wonder, and Surprise 82
    Betty Kane (Staley)
First Approach to Mineralogy 88
    Frederick Hiebel
"But Wickedness Has to Be in It, Too!" 94
    Georg Starke
Children's Quarrels 99
    Elisabeth Klein
The Challenge of Grades 7,8, and 9,
    with Special Reference to Art History 105
    Betty Kane (Staley)

III. THE HIGH SCHOOL

Modern Physics in the Waldorf High School 116
    Stephen Edelglass
The Human Skull: A Lesson with Grade Ten 118
    Francis Edmunds
Bookbinding in the High School 123
    Margaret Frohlich
A High School Course in Child Study 126
    Nanette Grimm
The Value of Art for the Adolescent 129
    A.W. Mann

Caterpillar Capacities:
   An Address to the Graduating Class 134
      Christy Barnes
Teaching Medieval Romances 139
      Jean Hamshaw
Mathematics in the Classroom:
   Mine Shaft and Skylight 142
      Amos Franceschelli
Grace at Meals: A Talk to the High School Students 151
      John Gardner

IV. THE WHOLE SCHOOL

Drawing: From First Grade to High School 156
      Carl Froebe
History Teaching, a Dramatic Art 168
      Henry Barnes
Biography in Education 175
      William Bryant
A Creative Approach to Language Teaching 181
      René Querido
The Waldorf School Movement in North America 193
      Francis Edmunds
Acknowledgments 201
Biographies of the Authors and Translators 202
Waldorf Schools of North America 210
World List of Waldorf/Rudolf Steiner Schools 218
Books on Waldorf Education 219
Contents of Waldorf Schools, Vol. I:
   Kindergarten and Early Grades 222
Index of Subjects, Authors, Translators 225

Introduction

The world was at war and our country would soon be drawn into it; the year was 1940. We could not guess that the atomic age was to be our future. But there were some who looked squarely at the present chaos, horror, and hopelessness, and realized that our children's education is at all times the most positive step to change what must be changed—and that a living spring of ideas, forbidden and imperiled throughout Europe, was available to schools and teachers searching for them here in America.

The first small Waldorf school on this continent had opened in New York City in 1928 with five teachers and 13 children and had struggled through the depression years. It grew slowly and painfully; a devoted body of parents and friends grew with it, finally forming themselves into the Rudolf Steiner School Association, whose aim was not only to support the school but also "to make this way of education known throughout the country"—by means of lectures and exhibitions of student work in the city, summer educational conferences at the Threefold Farm in Spring Valley. Aid for the suffering Waldorf schools, teachers and children in Europe—food, medicine, school supplies—would be stepped up, especially when the war ended and rebuilding was begun. In order to make all these activities known and, more importantly, to describe Waldorf education through the experience and writing of the teachers themselves, it would be necessary to publish a Bulletin.

Someone's happy inspiration named the Association's publication "Education as an Art"; the first number appeared in April 1940—it was to continue for 38 years without a pause. The first editor, Nancy Bartlett Laughlin, was followed by Mary Cross and then, until 1945, by Arvia MacKaye (Ege). By this time 400 members of the Rudolf Steiner School Association were receiving the Bulletin, and Hermann von Baravalle, Beulah Emmett, A.C. Harwood, teachers and parents of the school were sending in articles; and Vera Leroi reported on thousands of dollars collected for the "Milk Fund", which provided 500 children with a daily mug of hot milk, containing a homeopathic nerve medicine developed in Arlesheim, extra breakfasts also for teachers, paper, pencils, chalk, crayons, music supplies, and clothing, for many schools in Germany and Holland.

The school had moved by 1945 to the East Side, first renting the former Diller-Quaile Music School building on East 92st Street and then wildly-wonderfully purchasing the "magnificent mansion" on East 79th that is still the Elementary School. There were now more than a hundred students in eight grades and two kindergartens. There were three Waldorf schools besides the Rudolf Steiner School sponsoring the Educational Summer Conferences; Kimberton Farms School in Pennsylvania was founded in 1941; High Mowing School in New Hampshire in 1942: St. Hubert's School in Massachusetts had moved to this country from France when the war began but stayed only a few years in existence. The Executive Committee of the Rudolf Steiner School Association included Dr. Hermann Poppelbaum, Mary Halliday Mitchell, Virginia Paulsen, Henry Barnes, William Harrer, and Dorothy Jeffrey (Harrer).

In 1946 Christy Barnes, a class teacher in the school at that time, became editor, shaper, and inspirer of "Education as an Art"—a task she was to fulfill with rare tenacity and skill for thirteen years. Her editorial skill is evident in these two volumes, in articles by Margarethe Buehler, Christoph Boy, Frederick Hiebel, Elisabeth Klein, as well as by teachers at the New York school: Margaret Peckham, William Harrer, Karl Ege. In 1953 Virginia Paulsen became her assistant-editor.

By 1959 the president of the Rudolf Steiner School Association was Sonya Tamara Clark, a well-known foreign and war correspondent for the New York Herald Tribune; she was to remain head of the Association until its demise in 1969. Its only task now was the publishing of the Bulletin.

The subscription list grew steadily, especially with the founding of new schools: Green Meadow in Spring Valley (1950), Highland Hall in Los Angeles (1955), and the Sacramento Waldorf School (1959). Sonya Clark announced Christy Barnes' resignation "with regret . . . she has brought to our Bulletin the delightful imagination of the born writer. She has made it alive with ideas and pictures. Every issue was a small treasure for people interested in Waldorf education. We hope that she will continue to contribute to it."

Indeed she did! You will find an article on Choral Recitation by Christy Barnes in Volume I and a "Talk to a High School Graduating Class" in this volume; there were many more, published during her years of teaching at the Rudolf Steiner School, chiefly on speech, language, and literature. You will find others, written later for the "Journal for Anthroposophy", which she brought out as editor for eleven years. At the present, Christy Barnes runs the Adonis Press, which publishes a limited number of books and distributes supplies to Waldorf schools.

From 1959 on Ruth Pusch was the editor of "Education as an Art". During the '60s five of the American Waldorf schools agreed to publish the little bulletin—still only eight or twelve pages—on a co-operative basis. "This should bring to a wider audience the lively, vigorous immediacy of Rudolf Steiner's educational ideas. For the teachers and parents of each school there will be the added satisfaction of recognizing mutual efforts in many distant sections of the country. We may hope that all the Waldorf schools—even the tiny beginnings of schools—will gather some strength from this co-operative venture." Mohala Pua in Honolulu was one of these "beginnings" and we could soon record the opening of the first Canadian school in Toronto (as well as report on the first one in South Africa).

Finally, in 1969, "at the ripe age of 28", we announced that "Education as an Art" would be striding out into the world. It would no longer be published by the Rudolf Steiner School Association, which had outlived its usefulness, but by the Waldorf Schools of North America, working now together and meeting in an annual conference for mutual plans and decisions. The Detroit school had been founded in 1965—there were ten Waldorf schools on this continent! Every issue of "Education as an Art" listed them proudly inside the cover.

The following ten years brought steadily expanding Waldorf growth:

1969 Washington DC (now in Maryland)
1971 Great Barrington MA, Lexington MA,
      Baltimore MD, Vancouver BC
1972 Marin CA, Pine Hill NH
1973 Harlemville NY
1974 Summerfield CA, Chicago IL, Denver CO
1976 Santa Cruz CA

Efforts in other places, California, Hawaii, Michigan, Ohio, Oregon, Wisconsin and Canada were beginning to bear fruit.

The final number of the Bulletin, which followed Ruth Pusch's retirement, was assembled by an Editorial Board headed by Amos Franceschelli and included May Eliot (Paddock), Virginia Paulsen, Alan Howard, Ihor Radysh and Mel Belenson. It celebrated Fifty Years Waldorf Education in North America (1978/79), reminding us of those brave, resourceful pioneers of 1928.

Back in 1969, in the Winter issue of "Education as an Art", Alan Howard (who later became Associate Editor) wrote the lead article: "Then and Now: Fifty Years of Waldorf Education."

"When society through its democratically elected governments took over responsibility for education and made it public," [his article began], *"it took over at the same time responsibility for the spiritual and cultural welfare of mankind as a whole. Not many people, perhaps, realized it at the time, but certainly people are beginning to realize it now."*

There followed a description of the social chaos in Europe in 1919 and the question put to Rudolf Steiner by a group of Stuttgart businessmen, How can we create a better social future?

"His reply was unequivocal: you must start by doing something about education."

Emil Molt, one of those businessmen, made it possible to found the first Waldorf school, mother of all the hundreds of Waldorf schools in the world today. Alan Howard ended his article with words that can stand as the true introduction to this volume.

"And so one sees the future of Waldorf not as just the perpetuation of another 'method'. We could indeed well dispense with this overworked word 'method', except in those specific spheres where it properly belongs; for when all is said and done, the method is the teacher, and the teacher is a human being who believes in the invincible spirit in every person, and who seeks to bring it down from the realm of ideology into the everyday activity of public life, by looking for it and working with it in all those committed to his care.

"That, in the final analysis, is what Waldorf Education is; what it was; and what it must always be."

Spring Valley 1993   Ruth Pusch

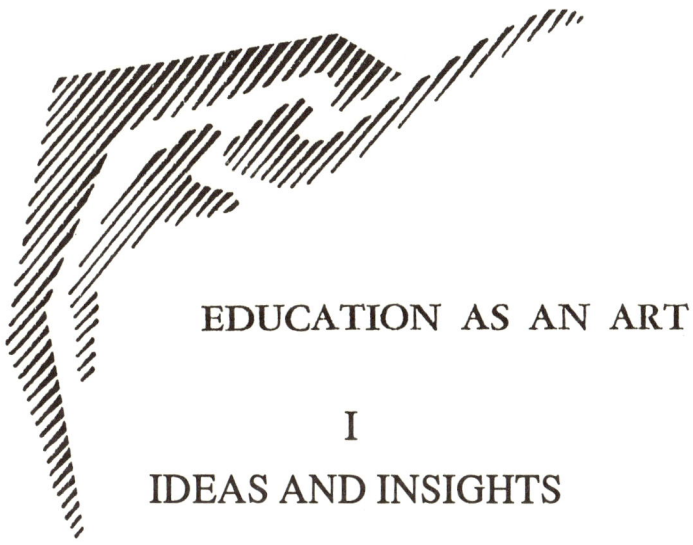

EDUCATION AS AN ART

I
IDEAS AND INSIGHTS

> Out of the gravity of our time
> There must be born
> Courage for deeds.
> Give to your teaching
> What the spirit has given you,
> And you will liberate mankind
> From the nightmare
> That weighs upon it
> Through materialism.
>
> Rudolf Steiner

(Translated from *Wahrspruchworte, Richtspruchworte, Sprüche und Widmungen*. Rudolf Steiner Nachlassverwaltung, 1953)

What Is So "Special" About The Waldorf Schools?

If you ask this of someone who is only slightly acquainted with the Waldorf schools, he will probably answer: that they lay particular stress on art—or that the children are not forever sitting at their desks—that they are always promoted to the next grade—that instruction is given in blocks, one subject at a time—that the children begin foreign languages on their very first day of school—that the actual learning to write and then read proceeds at a very slow pace—and much else of a similar nature.

This is all true; these are indeed some of the special features of the Waldorf schools. And yet all this tells very little about them. Almost every one of these characteristics has been met with before, in some form or other, in various forward-looking schools. Besides, all these things really belong to the external aspects of pedagogy. The fundamental character of the Waldorf schools can never be said to consist of external features alone.

An old school official of wide experience, who became well acquainted with the first Waldorf school in Stuttgart, said one day: "You people have something that puts you ahead of many other schools, private and public, and that is, that you try to base everything—without the slightest compromise—on the nature of the child himself."

That observation, of course, points to much more, to something more fundamental. It is true: in accepting children, the Waldorf schools do not consider their social or economic or racial or religious backgrounds, do not consider even their talents or special intelligence. Nor do the schools consider external goals toward which some children could be steered because of particular abilities (that is, not in the elementary grades). Every child is given all possible help—equally—to unfold by his own efforts whatever thinking-capacity is latent in him, and especially all the hidden heart qualities, as well as the will-forces and practical skills. The world today needs live personalities able to cope with present-day situations, so-called "real people" with creative talent and plenty of initiative—not just intelligent citizens molded to some standard.

But there again, it must be pointed out, the Waldorf schools do not stand alone—thank God! They know that in these aims they stand on common ground with the best and most independent educators of the day.

No,—there is still more that has to do with this "basing everything on the child himself." Its most important aspect has to be added to all this, if one wants to describe the intrinsic character of the Waldorf schools.

Those of us whose work is in these schools believe that through Rudolf Steiner and anthroposophy we have been able to build what we do on a deeper and broader *knowledge of the real being of the child* than can be found elsewhere today: an exact scientific knowledge, accessible to everyone, of childhood itself (and thus, the 'universal child'), of the successive periods of development, with their many variations of acceleration and slowness, of the interweaving of body, soul, and spirit, with the one-sidedness that is individually possible and the hindrances that may happen. And then, in addition, a knowledge of each individual child as he stands before us with his strengths and his weaknesses—strengths that arouse in him happy expectation of the life ahead of him, weaknesses that reveal his need of help, because he cannot cope with his difficulties alone.

It is in this striving for knowledge of the child-nature, of the 'universal child' and of each individual child who comes to us, that the true character of the Waldorf schools can be found. This is the foundation and also the justification for all the special features mentioned—and many more besides. They have not been adopted out of some pedagogical fancy; they follow by strong natural consequence the knowledge that has been attained of the child and child development.

However, this striving for knowledge in which the Waldorf School teachers involve themselves needs something to complete it, still something else. So much more could often be accomplished with the children, sometimes very much more, if the parents too would involve themselves more fully in their part of the task of their children's education—and theirs is the most important part—if they too would endeavor to grasp this fundamental knowledge. Then home and school would be working together in ever more lively co-operation, supporting each other, complementing each other. Together they would be shaping our schools into ever more beautifully rounded character and many-sidedness. The schools would then become stronger and more useful, for the benefit and the joy of those who have most to do with them: our children.

(1974) —Erich Gabert

Translated by Gladys Hahn from an article in "*Erziehungskunst: Monatsschrift zur Pädagogik Rudolf Steiners*", *December, 1958*, with the permission of the editor.

I wonder what you would say if you saw someone with a plate of fish in front of him, carefully cutting away the flesh and consuming the bones! You would certainly be afraid that the bones might choke him and that in any case he would not be able to digest them. On another level, exactly the same thing happens when we give the children dry, abstract ideas instead of living pictures, instead of something that engages the activity of the whole being.

Rudolf Steiner

At The Beginning

It was the summer of 1919 when, in the words of Rudolf Steiner, "the refreshing breeze of work for the Threefold Social Order was blowing through the streets and alleys of Stuttgart," and preparations for opening the Independent Waldorf School were going forward energetically.

One day Rudolf Steiner decided that since we were not progressing fast enough merely by writing letters, we must have someone travel about from place to place, to search out teachers who might be considered for the new school. And so E. A. Carl Stockmeyer, who was not too busy lecturing at the time, went off on a journey of discovery. He was supposed to gather together the "Stars," as Rudolf Steiner said, jokingly. However, as far as I can remember, the catch was a little meager. Most of the candidates for teaching at the Waldorf School came through a direct call from Dr. Steiner himself.

Stockmeyer's efforts were much more fruitful in connection with the school officials from whom we had to get a license. One must remember that this was a quite unusual situation: we wanted their permission for a new kind of school and their guarantee of complete freedom not only in the organization and administration, but also in every detail of our method.

Perhaps the fact that this new school did not fit into any ordinary category became a kind of protection for it—even a piece of good fortune. Dr. Heymann, the Director of Cultural Activities at that time, took charge of our petition with a surprising amount of good will. Rudolf Steiner had a leading part in all these negotiations, despite the other, truly gigantic demands on him. Later, he often said with evident satisfaction, "Indeed it was our great good luck at the time to slip through a mouse-hole that had been left open in the school laws of Wurttemberg. In this way we could make our entrance into life."

And now, after completing one preliminary after another, Rudolf Steiner could begin the educational course with his first lecture on the *Study of Man*, August 21, 1919. Everyone who had been invited to the course came together on that sunny August morning at a long table in the small "blue room" where, four months before, the first decision to found a school had been reached. The course participants stood singly or in small groups on both sides of the table, the light dimmed gently by the blue of the walls, tables and chairs. There was no lively conversation. Only the guests who had been invited were acquainted with each other; not many of the prospective teachers had met. Besides, everyone present was far too expectant in these decisive moments to enter into a conversation—or even to walk up and down in the room.

I, too, felt myself turning more towards an inner contemplation than to the outside. Beyond all question this was a moment of destiny to which everything on my path of life had been tending. It had led me to this place and now here, surely, were all those persons I had unconsciously sought. In what way would we be discovering and speaking to one another?

My mind was somewhat eased by the presence of two teachers whom I knew well, Carl Stockmeyer and Paul Baumann. At two others I had looked carefully during the general introductions that day, because Rudolf Steiner had spoken about them at the small preliminary meetings in the summer. One was Caroline von Heydebrand, of whom he had said humorously, "A tiny, piping voice, but a most gifted mind!" And immediately I recognized the truth of this description on meeting for the first time this small, dainty person with her clear and kindly glance.

The other was the Reverend Johannes Geyer, whose anthroposophical work in Hamburg Dr. Steiner had described to us. Johannes Geyer at that time was no longer the only churchman who found in anthroposophy the richest wellspring for his work. It was noteworthy that Geyer had now decided to come to the Waldorf School as a teacher and particularly that he did not consider this as a break with his former profession. From that time forward he gave himself for many years with great devotion to these new tasks.

Now at last, with the light step which at the same time always seemed consciously to feel the ground, Rudolf Steiner entered, went to his place at the head of the table, and with hardly a pause began his lecture. With him were Marie Steiner, Mieta Waller and Dr. Ludwig Noll.

Everyone had taken his place, and now I got my first full view of the man who was to become closest to me, both in life and in the spirit. It was the Austrian, Dr. Walter Johannes Stein, who was moving into the chair on my right with the perceptible vigor of a knight in armor leaping onto his horse. On my left was seated Paul Baumann.

With a few sentences Rudolf Steiner made an introduction in which there came to life a quite unusual, far from conventional festivity. We, the participants, received a welcome that also was completely unconventional and devoid of sentimentality. As he set out to render a general study of man, he welcomed us—I should like to say—by means of the very image of Man himself.

... The Waldorf educational movement has grown and spread out into all the world. For fifty years, searching, inquiring men and women have been trying to develop what was contained in that Pedagogical Course of 1919. But continually one is aware that everything as yet is only a beginning.

(1969) —Herbert Hahn

Translated from Herbert Hahn's autobiography *Der Weg, der mich führte* with the kind permission of the publisher, Verlag Freies Geistesleben, Stuttgart.

Twenty-four years ago Rudolf Steiner's most important educational course was published in English. It had been given to the first teachers of the first Waldorf School in Stuttgart, Germany, in the late summer of 1919, just a few weeks before that great pioneering venture opened its doors to the children of the workers in the Waldorf-Astoria Cigarette factory.
Cecil Harwood, himself one of the first teachers of the first Waldorf school in Great Britain, wrote the following report for Vol. 1, No. 2 (January, 1948) of "Child and Man", a magazine for Rudolf Steiner education published in England.* We are grateful for permission to reprint 'a brief gloss' that reminds us how challenging the ideas of this Study of Man were and still are.

Study Of Man

Rudolf Steiner's lectures to the teachers of the Waldorf School at its foundation have just been published in English under the above title. They deal with man as a threefold being of body, soul and spirit, and the human being is considered in turn from these three aspects. The lectures begin with a survey of man from the aspect of the soul, and I think that Dr. Steiner chose this entry both because childhood is essentially an experience of the soul, and because the soul, standing between the other two and drawing its experiences partly from the body and partly from the spirit, is the best gateway to an understanding of the trinity in human nature. The first lecture alone will convince anyone who reads it that there is here a psychology quite unlike anything which is taught in the modern world. In one sense the first lecture especially may be said to answer the question, What is education for? You may think of all the answers that might be given to that question by educators to-day; to make good citizens; or to make good men; or to fit a child to earn his

---

* See page 219, Books on education.

living; or to teach him to appreciate the cultural inheritance to which he is born. But when you have thought of them all (and they are very numerous) you will come nowhere near the answer which Dr. Steiner gave to the group of teachers who were about to receive the children into his first school. It is: to teach the children how to breathe properly. It is indeed an answer to take the breath away.

There are perhaps two interpretations of this advice which might be found in the world to-day. From the West would come the physical interpretation of such breathing exercises as are sometimes given even to quite young children; from the East would come the mystical interpretation of Yogi, by which the soul overcomes the body and wins spiritual experiences. Dr. Steiner does not mean either of these. He leads you instead into what might almost be called a meditation on breathing. Nor does this mean that you are to observe the process of breathing, though meditation might certainly include that. But observation takes you only through a series of processes. If you observe a leaf falling you follow its course from the tree to the ground, you notice the nature of its flight in the air, its color, texture, etc. But if you meditate on a falling leaf your mind will take you to all other experiences which have the same gesture or quality as the leaf in its fall. So it is with breathing. There are many processes in life which we do not call breathing, but which, in their essence, are as much breathing as the systole and diastole of the lung. For instance, joy and sorrow, laughing and weeping are a breathing of the soul—and become even a breathing of the body. We breathe out in joy, we go into an ecstasy, we stand outside ourselves. In sorrow we are contracted, we go into ourselves, we lose our connection with the outer world. Laughing empties our lungs, we laugh on the outbreath; but we cry on the inbreath; though it comes painfully and brokenly, we are always drawing our breath into our own lungs in the act of weeping. The children in the Bible complained to their companions that they had piped to them and they had not danced, and they had mourned with them and they had not wept. They could not understand those who did not enjoy the healthy breathing of the soul. The children who learn this breathing will draw their physical breath rightly as well, for the whole rhythmical system in man is the expression of the life of soul. In ancient times the soul could properly be approached through the body. It is one of the great changes in evolution that the body should now be approached through the soul.

Then there is the larger rhythm of night and day, which is a breathing both of the earth and of the soul. In the daytime children are breathing in their experiences; even sense perception is a form of breathing. But when they are asleep at night they take those experiences into the spiritual world where they breathe them out again. But the spiritual world cannot receive all experiences, and if the children bring into sleep things that it cannot accept, then comes something like a congestion of the outbreath. In waking life the physical body and the life forces are sustained and strengthened by high spiritual powers—those which in Christian terms are called the Archai and Archangels—but at night, when the soul leaves the body, this support is withdrawn. It is then a question of whether the Angel can sustain the thoughts and experiences which the soul takes with it into sleep. The old habit of saying a prayer before sleeping was meant to prepare the soul to bring the right thoughts into the spiritual world. But the most important thing is whether the children have gained during the day thoughts and pictures of the world which are acceptable to the spiritual powers who receive the soul in sleep. This form of outbreathing is conditioned by their parents and teachers.

A still greater rhythm of breathing is that of birth and death. Birth is incarnation, breathing in; death is excarnation, breathing out. Even physically the first breath we take is a breathing in, while the spirit leaves the body at death on the outbreath. It is natural, then, for a child to cry at birth, because it is an inbreathing process. If life is rightly lived, death should be the opposite. We should leave the body, not perhaps laughing, but at least with joy in our hearts. Sir William Jones, one of the early orientalists of the eighteenth century, has given the perfect expression to this double polarity of birth and tears, joy and death.

> On parent knees, a naked new-born child
> Weeping thou sat'st, while all around thee smiled.
> So live, that sinking to thy life's last sleep
> Calm thou may'st smile, while all around thee weep.

It is perhaps significant that it was an orientalist who wrote these lines, in which birth and death are united in such exquisite contrast. In the ancient East, and even into the age of the Greeks, birth was as much considered as death, and the incarnation of the soul was no less a part of common philosophy than its departure at death. Reincarnation was the foundation-stone of the Hindu conception of the soul, and Plato allows it to appear at the end of his greatest work, the *Republic*, in the culminating myth of Er, the soldier who was left for dead on the field of battle and on his recovery could describe how he had seen the journey of souls after death, and their choice of a new lot in life for their rebirth. It was one of the necessities of evolution that for many hundreds of years our thoughts about the soul should center only on the life after death, while life before birth was almost entirely disregarded. From the time of Christ this was true of pagan and Christian alike. The Emperor Hadrian did not speculate as to where his little wandering soul had come from; he was interested in where it was going to.

> *Animula vagula blandula,*
> *Hospes comesque corporis . . .*
> (Vital spark of heavenly flame!
> Quit, Oh quit this mortal frame . . .
>
>   (A. Pope)

But the Christian preoccupation with death rather than birth became more and more marked. By the fifteenth century men were giving all their wealth to endow chantries where mass might be said in perpetuity for the good of their souls; and though in the new age there were some sensitive spirits who experienced their own birth and childhood as a process of "coming down"—the mystics and poets like Traherne and Vaughan—the great preoccupation with death continued, and every other hymn of the nineteenth century ended with a reference to death (*piano*) and (*fortissimo*) to the entry of the soul into Heaven.

This was a necessity in the age when man was finding his ego through the experience of life on earth. But there was a real egotism in thinking that my duty on earth is to prepare myself for eternal happiness in heaven. Philosophically also the preoccupation with death lent strength to the view that the mind at birth is a *tabula rasa*, that man is born out of nothing and acquires all his experiences through sense perception—a view which lies behind the method of all modern natural science. But if birth is looked on as the high moment of incarnation and reincarnation (though this is in itself a gradual process) quite other views will be taken of life. You live in order to make good past misdeeds, to pay back to others what you owe, you share in the responsibility for the conditions of life which you find on the earth. And it will make a great difference, not only to you, but to the whole spiritual world what thoughts and impulses you take with you through the gate of death no less than through the gate of sleep. You make the balance between past, present and future.

Then from a right consideration of birth and death you will come to a new psychology, where the dimensions of time reveal themselves in their true relation to the soul. Most people imagine that they live only in the present, that the past is something which has disappeared and the future is something which does not exist. It is true that certain schools of thought are questioning this view today, but their speculations have not yet had much influence on practical psychology. But the truth is that powers from the past and from the future are always flowing into the soul at every moment of our lives. Every time we *think*, we are using powers which flow into our life from before birth. If we are not really able to think about the future at all except (as we all do) in terms of the past, it is because the forces of thinking itself flow in from the world before birth. But every time we *will* we are calling into ourselves forces from the future. That is why our deeds of will carry their effects so far beyond themselves. *Thinking* has an image character, it is reflection, it is something which we breathe in from before birth. *Willing* has a seed character, it draws the future into itself, as the seed draws the forces which will build and form the flower. When we will, we commit ourselves to the stream which flows on beyond our death. Between the two poles lies the realm of *feeling*, the essential kingdom of the soul. So that in each moment of life the soul breathes in and breathes out the past and the future. It is a rich experience.

With such thoughts as these Rudolf Steiner inaugurated the *Study of Man* for the teachers of his first school. Perhaps this brief gloss on the breathing of man will encourage some readers to study the lectures for themselves. They will discover what it is to conceive of man again as a microcosm reflecting in himself all the forces and powers of the universe—"in action how like an angel, in apprehension how like a God, the beauty of the world, the paragon of animals."

(1972)   A. C. Harwood

The Community Sense In Child And Adult

Every adult must often have had the experience of looking at young children and thinking wistfully: "If we could only, as adults, hold on to this wonderful responsiveness, this boundless trust in our fellow men, this consuming interest in everything around us, how different the world would be! Why can't we keep these qualities beyond early childhood?

What happens to them? Why does growing up seem to have to mean a deterioration from this cosmic purity of social-moral impulse which is the possession of every baby at birth?"

Actually the loss of these traits and others like them is no more to be regretted than the loss of our milk teeth, which are pushed out to make way for another set far more suited to adult mouths and needs. But here the analogy ceases, for Mother Nature plainly fails to provide us with a second set of social-moral powers. If she did, we should never be able to take the crowning human step to free, individual, social creativity. Our natural evolution carries us to the point of individuality, but there it leaves us. Any further steps must be taken by ourselves as free creators of a community life that could not come into being without our effort. We must ourselves find the way beyond the stage of rampant individualism, to which we are brought without our own doing, to mature cooperation with our fellow human beings.

Let us trace the growth pattern of the individual from birth to adulthood in order to consider education's role in helping him achieve full stature as a social being.

The family into which the baby enters at birth is his first community experience. He feels himself in a closely knit natural circle, and he is as organically at home in it as a seedling in its native soil. It would not occur to him to criticize or reject this community, no matter what its lacks. Yet very soon he senses the tensions that inevitably exist there. He overhears quarrels between older brothers and sisters and, perhaps, his parents. At once he reflects his concern, and a deep uneasiness lays hold on him. The magic circle has broken, even if only for a moment, and his belief in its safe wholeness is lastingly undermined. From now on he knows that even the most perfect of home paradises is continually threatened by potential serpents of dissension.

By the time he has become a schoolboy he has already developed sufficient independence to want to replace the narrow and vulnerable community of his family with a broader, freer one which he unconsciously hopes will prove more satisfying: the community of children. But in the company of his peers new shocks await him. There are frequent savage clashes of personality. He seeks aid and comfort in aligning himself with congenial groups which band against others. But now a new danger threatens: the world of boys and girls splits wide apart. Suddenly he becomes aware that there are two sexes, and he is a member of only one of them. The other sex withdraws to ever remoter, more mysterious distances. Now he really begins to be lonely and afraid.

Friendships become increasingly deep and important at this period. Yet it will be his experience that even his dearest friend differs from and with him in a thousand ways. He is hurt and bewildered in his search for a whole community by discrepancies in feeling and opinion. If he cannot think and feel exactly as his friends do, how can they be at one? For a time he recklessly adopts their viewpoints, only to realize with increasing maturity that he must find his own ground and stand upon it, or he is lost.

Now evolution has completed its task in him. He finds the strength and need to be his own friend, though secretly a very lonely young man. He begins to explore all the joys and solaces of being an individual. A certain aggressiveness is apt to awaken in him which makes him overplay his role and feel ridiculous. And all the time something vital is missing which he knows exists, though he may never find it: full community with other free and mature individuals.

Even in the best of cases this period is one of long duration, and it leads to great suffering in those of high ideals and sensitivity.

Education can profoundly affect the course of the individual's progress on this social via dolorosa, lessening its necessary suffering while preparing him in the end to reach his goal.

Two ways have been tried in the main: the meagre one of "practicing democracy" in committees, discussion, and individual expression of opinion, and that other which seeks to educate to community through making use of the creative arts as a prime trainer of the social impulses and capacities. Rudolf Steiner schools have made significant contributions to this latter striving.

Teachers in such schools recognize creativity to be the most central core of the human ego. They are therefore especially concerned with its development. Leaving the life of thought and reason for intensive cultivation at a later stage, they devote themselves in the primary and intermediate grades to fostering the life of feeling, the sense of beauty and proportion. Rhythm, color, stories, poetry, music, modeling, design and dramatics—these are the avenues through which all learning is first brought into the child's experience. Every subject is made to yield its rich content of meaning in artistic form.

In all such experience the group rather than the individual is paramount. In eurythmy, for example, the emphasis is upon patterns of movement. In recitation the speaking is choric. In music all participate in every song and instrumental composition. Individuals may have their single parts to perform, as in a drama, but these must have relation to the whole. Such communal experiences of creating beauty are freely and joyfully engaged in, and they are in their very nature prototypes of the highest conceivable form of free, creative social relationships.

The very way classes are organized encourages the growth of a sense of community, for in these schools the teacher customarily advances with a class from grade to grade, giving the group a stable center and imbuing its work at the different elementary levels with unity and organic sequence.

A further very important means of social education is the emphasis laid upon man in every study. Every subject, no matter how objective, begins, and is summed up, with its relationship to the human being in mind. Acoustics in the sixth grade, for example, first concerns itself with providing experiences of beauty in great works of music and poetry, and, after an extensive exploration of the laws of sound, ends with a study of the human ear. Man and animal, in the fourth grade, begins with a study of the wonderful balance and non-specialization of the human organism which permits man to be a free creator, as no animal can be, and ends with a picture of the human being as the whole animal kingdom resolved into a single harmonious and perfect form. Grammar, beginning in the second grade, is throughout an exploration of the relationship of the parts of speech to the structure and capacities of human beings, as, for instance, finding nouns to be the concept or head element in sentences; verbs, as doing-words, to be the limbs; adjectives, as words of feeling, to be the heart and breathing organism, etc. So the children learn, not through direct moral teaching, but in the impressions they receive of the glorious potentialities built into every facet of man's nature, to revere this being in themselves and others, to sense how much we have been given to work with if we but accept our creative role in Nature's hierarchy.

The child whose education has thus built up in him a profound respect for human beings, which has fostered his creative powers and enabled him to drink deep of the joy of group creating, will be person and artist enough to desire, envision, and help bring into being truly healthy forms of society.

Such a personality eventually grows beyond the limitations of narrow individualism to a sense of identification with the whole human race. For in learning to understand our own creative striving, we become aware of the striving of others and feel our kinship with it. We begin to be more and more keenly conscious of our responsibilities toward our fellow strivers. And in our association with others we realize that group enterprises offer opportunities not open to us as a single individual. We see in the group a number of others who, like ourselves, long to become more effective in their common task.

Here immense perspectives open. Not only does a really unified group of free individuals working together in a common cause offer us the possibility of full self-realization through its receptiveness toward our fruitful ideas and creative impulses, which are then often seen in a larger light than we perhaps first saw them; it challenges us to put forth that understanding effort toward others in the circle which gradually releases and makes use of individual potentiality in all its members. A new element comes into being: that of group creativeness, which transcends in depth and power the creativity of the single personalities which comprise it. Through the loving labor of our colleagues and ourselves there is born in the end that genuine social substance which is our own and the world's deepest need today.

(1947) Marjorie Spock

Principles And Growing Human Beings
From an address delivered before a meeting of high school principals

Although I am listed as a speaker against the plan of "indoctrination" of pupils, you will not expect me to speak against democratic ideals as such. Indeed I am convinced that they arise from the very core of human nature. The recognition of "the inalienable rights of man" is a human feature just as well as the use of fire or the upright posture of the body. The question before us, however, is not whether democratic ways of life are desirable ideals which we ought to foster in the young generation—our problem is whether we can implant these ideals in the manner often advocated, namely, by teaching them as principles of conduct.

It is here that I ask to be allowed to disagree. My objection springs from pedagogical facts experienced over and over again. *One cannot implant abstract principles into growing human beings by simply teaching them as principles.* The mentality of the child and the adolescent, widely different from that of the adult, simply does not allow this. The child's mentality as described by the best knowers of our time asks for living imagery, as nature herself offers it. It grasps everything within the "fringe," as William James called it, of their living relations, never as isolated objects. The child experiences the human being, not in abstracto, but as the living presence of this or that man or woman—never as an incorporation of principles, however dear these may be to the grown-up. Thus when we want principles to be present in the adult we must not inoculate the child. We must take the laborious way of first preparing the matrix or ground on which such principles may later grow. Principles are not seeds to be put into the child, they are rather fruits which will appear in the future. When this fruit is gathered, the teacher may long since have passed away.

What, then, can we do to prepare children to become producers of sound human principles later in life, principles of human value and dignity, of freedom and inalienable rights? Instead of teaching ideals we must mold every subject taught so as to bring forth in the young soul an alive, rightly colored picture of the whole human being. All our efforts, in whatever subject, must be centered on this point. It is futile to try to teach the appreciation of human values as a distinct subject along with others, just as we cannot give separate lessons in character formation. The human touch must adhere to everything we bring before the child. Every single subject must become man-centered, if you allow the term. That this is possible has been practically shown. I shall give some examples of this in a moment.

The point is that if our teaching has this touch upon it, the adults who go forth from our schools will know what they mean when speaking of humanity. They will have a deep appreciation of human values which no anti-human propaganda can take away from them.

It is in this matter of doing preparatory work for post-school life that the average school has failed. This has been said here with emphasis so I need not prove it. But I should like to ask: could anything else be expected, when science in our age is what it is? How can we expect the teacher to convey to his pupils a feeling of the human kernel in all knowledge, when science itself is lacking this very kernel? If we are to accuse we have to go to the seats of learning, to those who set the tasks of modern inquiry. But we are not here to accuse. We want to understand. It was under the influence of natural science that research was directed less toward man himself than toward everything around him. Modern research is most tragically lacking a focus towards which all investigation should converge. This focus is the human entity in all its ramifications. Biology alone cannot solve this task. Psychology by itself cannot do it because it has made the borderline between man and animal indistinct. As to psychoanalysis, it gets stuck half-way, entangled in neurotic problems and, when proceeding to the study of the child, poisons the atmosphere of inquiry with cunning suspicion.

From the places of higher learning the teacher of today receives the distorted picture of the child: as a little animal not yet human, with wicked and hidden cravings which have to be curbed or replaced by better strivings: an empty sack to cram knowledge into. He is not given the picture of the child as a living and ensouled individuality entrusted to the teacher's care. He has received no concept of what the mature human being really is. How can he give convincing weight to his words in speaking of human values while science continues to tell him that a person is only a chance product sprung from the tip of the animal tree? How can he convey to the child in his care a feeling that a mature human being is an aim worth striving for when, at the back of his mind, he has the notion that there is no real totality "humankind"—but only a number of sub-types each of which has come from another anthropoid ape in another climate?

Knowledge of man has first to be restored to its due place. Then it will provide the teacher with a firm foundation of facts upon which to base his description of the whole human being. And such a new knowledge of man is there since Rudolf Steiner gave it. It is possible, now, to present the human being as a comprehensive and archetypal form of which the higher animal forms are deviations. In a pictorial way such a truth can be given to the youngest child so that he can grasp it with his feelings. Such an idea sinks deeply into the soul and mind and will make him regard every one else differently when he grows up. Gradually the picture transforms itself into the idea that man is an aim to strive for. There is no need for us to set up abstract ideals before him, straw puppets stuffed with dry principles of goodness.

With the adolescent the task of the teacher changes, not in substance but in shade. The growing boys and girls want to see in their teacher the living, breathing example of humanity. All depends now upon his living up to this expectation. In this he will set the standard for their concept of the human being. If successful, the moral faculties in the pupils are furthered. If not, he not only disappoints them, but saps their future moral strength. Teachers who are dry explainers, absent-minded savants or cold pedants are obnoxious enough, but at least as harmful are the vague and abstract idealists.

From the way in which the teacher appreciates human dignity and capacity there springs up in the pupil's later life a conscious understanding of social necessities and of inalienable human rights. A formulation of such ideals may be latent in the adolescent so that when he hears or reads about them he will at once feel that these are of his innermost concern. We need not preach to him a doctrine which we have worked out in definitions. The living example he saw will have done its work. He recognizes consciously what he has learned to love and he knows it is worth living and dying for.

The lure of the demagogue who uses the trick of discrediting his opponents has no power over such a man or woman. They will never take brutality for force, nor emotional speeches for signs of greatness, nor will they fall victim to cheap illusions concerning the rottenness of intelligence or the glorious achievements of hatred. They will recognize the mean fanatic even in the disguise of the demagogue who poses as a world-savior. They will reject the paradise he promises because they do not want to live as mental slaves, however well catered to. They will refuse the offer of having the future of numerous children assured, because they would have to pay for it with the sacrifice of freedom. They will never sign a declaration of dependence.

We do not speak of a dream here but of successful work done in Europe in two decades of school practice. Children in these Rudolf Steiner schools have taken up in early years, in picture form, what we have termed here as man-centered knowledge. Through years in succession they have experienced the enthusiastic presentation of human development through the ages of history, culminating in the fight for freedom. They have taken up the ineffaceable impressions of man discovering fire, or of the Roman hero burning his hand in the face of his accusers. They have heard and have recited with enthusiastic hearts the words of the 4th of July, 1776, that all men are created equal and that they are endowed by their Creator with certain inalienable Rights, and that among these are Life, Liberty, and the pursuit of Happiness.

Men and women who have had such an education will not have been "indoctrinated," but they will have ripened the seed implanted in them at school.

(1969)   Dr. Hermann Poppelbaum

Some Characteristics of Steiner Education

A Radio Interview on WNYC
June 18, 1956

Mr. GRAVINA: This afternoon we shall learn something about Rudolf Steiner, whose name some of you may already know. Steiner lived at the turn of the century. He was a most important philosopher and one of the most creative thinkers of his time. He came from Austria. I read recently that, as a result of Steiner's philosophy and his teaching, more than sixty schools bearing his name are now established in various parts of the world.

I thought you might enjoy speaking with the chairman of the faculty of the Rudolf Steiner School here in New York, Mr. Henry Barnes, who is our guest this afternoon.

There are of course, Mr. Barnes, some basic differences in the educational concept of the Rudolf Steiner schools and that which we associate with the ordinary public schools in America, and perhaps elsewhere in the world. Do you think we might begin by trying to distinguish between the two approaches to education?

Mr. BARNES: First of all I'd like to say that all good teachers who are sincere teachers in their fields have a great deal in common, but I do think that there are differences between the Rudolf Steiner school and other schools, including the public schools. They range from more fundamental questions of point of view to practical questions of administration and of method.

One of the differences in administration is that each Rudolf Steiner school is administered by its faculty. This means that every teacher shares in the responsibility for the administration of the school and has to learn to deal with questions which face any school administrator and to take responsibility for the school as a whole.

Mr. GRAVINA: The faculty actually shares ownership of the school?

Mr. BARNES: In the case of the Rudolf Steiner school in New York, that is true. But this varies from school to school. Each Steiner school is quite independent of the others and each school is set up in a way that is most practical for the country and the situation in which it finds itself. Another very fundamental difference is that in the elementary school we follow the principle that the same teacher who begins with a group of children in the first grade stays with them in their main lesson subjects throughout the whole course of the elementary school.

Mr. GRAVINA: That is quite an innovation.

Mr. BARNES: That it is, and it is one that I know is often startling to people when they hear it for the first time. Immediately the question comes up: Well, suppose they get a bad teacher? And that is a very understandable query. But our experience is that if you do stay with one group of children you get to know them better than you could ever do in a single year. At the end of the first year you feel that you are only just ready to begin to go to work with them. If you also know that you are going to face problems which you may or may not solve now—if you are going to face those problems later you have the greatest possible incentive to try to meet them now and not simply shelve them, as is so often the case.

Mr. GRAVINA: It seems to me that it has the advantage of keeping the teacher interested also, which is not always the case in the other system.

Mr. BARNES: That's right. I think that a teacher who stays with the same group of children cannot get into a rut, in the way that a teacher who teaches the first grade year after year might easily do. You grow with your children. You have the excitement of exploring new fields of knowledge with them. You are faced with new subject matter, which of course means that you have to prepare yourself each year anew. This may be strenuous, but it certainly is rewarding. In our school the children also have contact with many other teachers during the course of the day—but this class teacher teaches them their basic academic subjects. These are taught in a long, two hour lesson at the beginning of the day while the children are freshest and least distracted. We try then to schedule the non-academic work—the more active physical and artistic work—later in the day.

Mr. GRAVINA: While you're on the subject of the administrative technique used in the Rudolf Steiner school—in New York, at least, Mr. Barnes—I understand that your school functions without a principal in the ordinary sense.

Mr. BARNES: That is true. We consider the administration as centered in the faculty itself. All basic questions of school policy are brought to the faculty for decision. This doesn't mean that everybody does everything. Too many cooks would certainly spoil the broth. But the Chairman of the Faculty is elected by the faculty for whatever period of time the faculty wishes him to act, and he acts as the representative of the faculty and not as an administrator imposed upon it.

Mr. GRAVINA: That seems logical . . . Thus far we've been talking about *how* you teach. I think perhaps our listeners are curious now to know something about *what* you teach. What do you see as the goal of education for the students who come to the Rudolf Steiner school?

Mr. BARNES: That of course is a big question but I think that fundamentally our goal would be that the inherent individuality which exists in every human being, with his gifts and his limitations, shall come to the fullest possible expression. That implies that each individual must have a chance to receive an all-round education, that not only his gifts shall be fostered but his weaknesses shall be strengthened, and that, in the end, as an adult he shall be able to make the best possible use of the particular gifts and talents which he has.

Mr. GRAVINA: Can you give us any examples of how you try to accomplish this?

Mr. BARNES: One way in which we work is through a very carefully integrated curriculum which extends right through the full twelve grades of elementary and high school. It is our aim in the elementary school to bring to the children an introduction to each of the basic branches of knowledge, so that, for instance, in history, beginning in the fifth grade, we give the students first an introduction to the earliest beginnings of history—going way back into the pre-Christian cultures—and bringing them as far as the end of the Grecian period in the fifth grade. In the sixth grade that is continued with the study of Rome and the early Middle Ages; in the seventh grade, with the period of the Renaissance and the Age of Discovery; and in the eighth grade we bring them right up to the present day.

We also try to give them a broad introduction to the sciences, starting in the sixth grade with an introduction to physics, with geometry and algebra, and continuing in the seventh grade with physics, an introduction to chemistry and physiology, and concluding in the eighth grade with a general summary of the sciences which have been introduced to them in the earlier grades.

Then this is all taken up again in high school so that what they learned in the elementary school in terms of picture, narrative and biography, in a more elementary fashion, is then studied anew and the effort is made to get them to understand the laws which are at work behind the phenomena and the stories of history, and behind the phenomena of science.

Mr. GRAVINA: From time to time, Mr. Barnes, as I'm sure you know, we read in our papers and we learn from our friends—many of whom are parents—that the question of the spiritual values comes up quite often in relation to the education system, although I must say that in the majority of cases it never seems to go beyond the stage of "Should a prayer be recited at the beginning of the school day" or "Should students be released for religious training elsewhere?"

Mr. BARNES: I think this is one of the most important questions with which we are faced in American education today, and of course it does go back to what one's basic conception of a human being is. If one thinks of a human being as just a chance happening in the universe who has no meaning and no destiny, then one will teach him in one way. But if you have the conviction that a human being is more than that, and that there is in every human being something that is essentially spiritual, one will then present everything which one brings to the children from that point of view. One of the concepts which we feel is fundamental to the good education is the idea of the dignity of the human being—that there is a dignity inherent in man which distinguishes him from the animals and from the other kingdoms of creation, and we do our best to awaken—especially in the little children—a real sense of respect and reverence for older people, for the material world, for the world of nature, and for the world of a higher order which has created them and which has created the world in which they live. We feel that that basic attitude toward life—which is one of respect and gratitude—is then transformed into a capacity for a positive, undivided ability to live in the world, and to act without fear and without hesitation. Rudolf Steiner once made the very interesting remark that hands which have learned to pray in childhood can bless in old age.

Mr. GRAVINA: That's a wonderful statement . . . We know of course that the public schools in a general sense have faced, and are facing, a serious shortage of teaching personnel. What has been your experience in attracting good teachers to private schools such as the Steiner School?

Mr. BARNES: I believe that a good teacher is born and that any teacher who really wants to teach is an idealist. The fundamental motive that will either bring him into teaching or will keep him out of it is not so much the salary—although of course he has to have a salary sufficient to live on—but is whether or not he feels that his creative capacities can truly come to expression in his profession. If he feels that in becoming a teacher he is going to be limited in what he can do, if he is going to be so systematized that he has no opportunity to do a creative job in his own work, then the creative person is going to stay out of the profession.

If on the other hand he sees the possibility of doing a pioneer job—and every teacher's job is really a pioneer job—it is always a new beginning with every child—then the person with pioneer initiative will come into teaching in spite of the fact that the salaries are not what they ought to be. I don't want to argue that the salary shouldn't be much better than they are.

Mr. GRAVINA: Well, this is probably the first time that many people are hearing of the point of view that the teacher shortage can be explained in terms other than low pay: the possible lack of creative goals for teachers.

We've been talking about the schools in some detail, Mr. Barnes, and I realize we haven't said much about the man who is responsible for this development—Rudolf Steiner himself. I think our audience might enjoy hearing something about the kind of man he was and also something of his varied interests.

Mr. BARNES: Although I never had the opportunity of meeting him personally—from all that I know of him I think that he must have been a most extraordinary person and certainly he has had a very far-reaching influence on his day. His lifework has touched a great many different fields. There is a movement in agriculture, known as bio-dynamic agriculture, which derives directly from indications which he gave to farmers. There are a great many doctors who are working in the field of medicine with ideas which he gave. And as you have already mentioned, there are over sixty schools now which are either called Rudolf Steiner schools or in some way directly owe their existence to the initiative and the ideas which he stood for.

Mr. GRAVINA: Did some of these schools actually come into existence while he was still alive?

Mr. BARNES: Yes. The first school of this kind was founded in Stuttgart, Germany, in 1919, immediately after the first World War, and Rudolf Steiner was asked to found that school and to direct it. That is the school known as the Free Waldorf School, founded by a man by the name of Emil Molt, who was the owner of the Waldorf-Astoria cigarette factory. He was a very far-sighted industrialist and realized that the end of the "hard times" had not yet come and that the new generations which were coming were going to have to face conditions even more difficult than those they had just gone through in the first World War. He wanted to do something of fundamental value for those people, and he asked Steiner whether he would be willing to found a school for the children of the workers in his factory. Steiner agreed, on the condition that it would not be restricted to any one group, economically or socially, and that he be entirely free of all external control, economic, political, or religious, to build up the school as he saw fit. That was the beginning of the Waldorf school movement, or the Rudolf Steiner educational movement that we know today.

Mr. GRAVINA: And certainly a marvelous example of the kind of enlightened cooperation you could have between industry and education.

Mr. BARNES: That I think is something which we have yet to see developed in this country, although I do know that leading industrialists are realizing that their biggest potential resource is not material but is human, and that if they do not reinvest some part of their profits in conserving and developing this human resource, then industry itself is also going to fail.

Mr. GRAVINA: Of course there has been and is a tremendous movement on the part of many organizations, including business groups, toward the scholarship technique, and that is praiseworthy; and yet if we have to question the basic educational method itself, it becomes a matter of deciding where efforts, time and money should be best spent.

Mr. BARNES: Yes. And I think there is another question involved there and that is one of specialization. A great deal is said today about the need for engineers and for scientists, and the point of view is taken that if you have better science courses and specialize sooner in the scientific branches of knowledge you are going to get better scientists. I think this is a fundamental mistake. I think that the best scientist is the best and most creative thinker and the best all-around individual, and that the task of education is first of all to educate human beings, who can then become scientists. As long as industry limits its support to technical schools, where they hope to get a direct benefit as a result of the money they have spent, I think they are not going to accomplish the goal which they hope to accomplish.

Mr. GRAVINA: How good a chance do we have in the near future, Mr. Barnes, of bridging the gap in educational thinking and concepts that exists now between the system used at the Steiner schools and those used in the public schools?

Mr. BARNES: Of course the private school, or independent school, has one great advantage and that is that it *is* independent, and is therefore able to adapt itself to new ideas more completely and more quickly than any big system such as the public school system. But I think that the source of education is the same for the public school teacher as it is for the private school teacher. That source is a knowledge of the human being, and to the extent that they draw their inspiration from the same source the results limited by the difficulties of working in a big system can be applied equally well in either field—because a good teacher is a good teacher in whatever kind of a school he teaches.

Of Machines And Men

When Plato likened man's task in life to that of a charioteer driving a chariot drawn by a white and a black horse of different inclinations and temperaments, he presented to mankind an archetypal image which is still full of vital significance for our times. And when Sir C. P. Snow signaled that humanity is dividing into two cultures, one humanistic and one technological, without mediation, he was, in fact, describing Plato's white and black horses. Unfortunately, Snow was insufficiently aware of the third force, which can and must take charge as a charioteer at all times: the wisdom of man, "anthropos-sophia."

Our time tends to be dominated by problems which arise from an awareness in terms of absolute contrasts. Issues are defined in terms of:

pleasing others versus pleasing oneself
black power versus white power
public schools versus private schools
fundamentalists versus evolutionists,

to name a few examples.

Our national examining and testing effort admits only answers of 'true' or 'false,' though not rarely are 'wrong' answers merely proof of a superior insight on the student's part. Indeed, it may become necessary to impart to bright students, along with a real education, a special course in test-taking, the skill of interpreting questions without profundity or originality.

Thinking in terms of true or false, make or break, fail or safe, etc. is justified in the realm of technology. Our digital computers operate on the often repeated alternatives of zero or one.

Thus a conceptual climate is generated in which people also tend to be regarded in similar terms: You are 'turned on' or 'turned off.' When this kind of thinking penetrates into education there is cause for concern.

In educational psychology today the country listens in the main to two schools of thought. A more or less humanistic school, usually with strong Freudian overtones, of which J. S. Bruner may be viewed as a prominent representative, versus a mechanistic school, usually with a strongly behavioristic outlook, of which B. F. Skinner is probably the best known exponent. Looking at this state of affairs one is reminded again and again of Plato's white and black horses, and one wonders: Where is the charioteer, the truly wise human guidance?

Here Waldorf schools, based on the educational psychology of Rudolf Steiner, have a real contribution to make. Their entire effort is permeated by a striving to recognize in each child and in each issue the charioteer. His growth is fostered; his integrity, his freedom, and his creativity are cultivated, so that he may find his way through life not only with skill and understanding but also with deep joy.

* * *

In our country with its high standard of living, children as well as adults are constantly surrounded by machines and technology. Seldom do we give serious thought to the question whether and how these affect us. Machines are thought of as instruments for affecting our environment so as to suit our needs, not as affecting us ourselves. And yet they do tend to affect people of all ages profoundly and often adversely, and children even more so than adults. What are these effects? And how can one neutralize them?

My primary concern is not with effects which stem from faulty technology, such as: impairment of hearing due to industrial noise; diseases and deaths caused by air pollution or by the addition of unsuitable chemicals to food; or cancer or genetic damage caused by an accumulation in time of the effects of small doses of ionizing radiation emitted by TV sets. Much well-documented research has been published about such effects—and is widely ignored. The causes for this type of effect can be recognized on a purely technical level. By designing machines better, with more sophisticated insight into human physiology, these causes can, in principle, be eliminated. It is true that many casualties will probably have to occur before enough pressure is built up to force industry to reckon more conscientiously with the well-being of the population; but my primary concern is with problems that are *inherent* in the human use of machines, problems which, by their very nature, cannot be eliminated by technical improvements.

Our organism has evolved through long ages under relatively stable environmental conditions on earth. Our bodily functions as well as the functions of our mind have become attuned to these conditions. We have developed internal biological clocks which more or less synchronize our waking-sleeping cycle to the diurnal period of twenty-four hours. Our physiology makes profound adjustments to the seasons. We could not live on earth in our present form if the average temperature were a mere hundred degrees hotter or colder. We could not survive if the flow of sense impressions ('signals') that goes with our normal activities were many times greater than it is at present. Nor could we properly survive if our internal and external bodily movements were subjected to severe restrictions.

It is part of the nature of our journey on earth that our body and mind are attuned so as to operate, within certain tolerances, around a certain balance between meaningful bodily activity and corresponding sense impressions: a balance between motor and sense activity. The circulatory system functions prominently in maintaining this balance, and our entire life of feelings is closely connected with this balance. Indeed, happiness and health are rarely found where this balance is upset.

The crux of the problem of our machine age is that machines tend to upset this balance, by reducing the bodily activity that corresponds to certain sensory impressions. How little do we move our body while riding in a car, and how many 'signals' do we receive during such a ride! How much do we feed into our senses when watching TV while our body is completely inactive!

How does human nature react to this type of imbalance? The senses become dulled, the person becomes inattentive, restless, and nervous. He finds it more and more difficult to concentrate, consequently he achieves little, yet he never has time nor interest for undertaking anything. He may become apathetic, and often develops circulatory or heart trouble after a while. Teachers with some experience in these matters can easily tell the TV addicts from those who do not watch TV habitually, by their different attention in class. The 'hectic' pace of life that kills so many adult hearts is not hectic because so much bodily activity is required but because so much immobility, coupled with sensory overload, is imposed upon us.

The Amish communities live practically without machines, but to advocate a return to this mode of life for all of us would set the clocks back. No amount of persuasion in some such direction can hope for more than fringe support. We may admire from a distance people like Rousseau or Thoreau for their feeling for nature and for their strong individualism, but we cannot honestly expect that a majority of our contemporaries in the Western world will follow their example. The question is rather: What can be done so as to keep the real benefits which our technological age affords, while eliminating its adverse effects?

The Rudolf Steiner schools have directed themselves for decades to such questions and have some very significant answers to offer.

* * *

Rudolf Steiner built his educational philosophy on his own extensive teaching experience as an educator working under a wide variety of circumstances, as well as on an encompassing fund of knowledge of earlier educational ideas before him. He concludes that the learning experiences of a child must always provide a balance between the human sense-pole and the action-pole. And this balance can only be attained if all school activities are permeated by the arts. Not only the audio- and visual arts, but also, and especially, the art of movement known as 'eurythmy.' The arts should be integrated with other subjects, so as to permeate these with creativity and beauty. In this sense all of education must literally become an art.

This type of education awakens and strengthens the 'charioteer' in the child. It allows the inner life to unfold in its own way and to draw enrichment from experience. It leads to purposeful self-control, and thus to the control of one's environment. Whatever is learned in an artistic way will not become rigid like a bouquet of plastic flowers. It should be flexible and subject to growth and further development throughout life. This kind of learning rests on 'empathy' of the child towards what is being learned, and on a teacher-child relation that is sustained by mutual empathy.

Here we touch a sensitive nerve of current educational psychology. Responses to stimuli, such as are required for tests of all kinds, *can* be acquired without affecting that deep inner life-level from which empathy springs. I doubt whether empathy, the complete surrender (for a short time) to what one observes, the identification with another person or being, can be tested. It is infinitely varied and subtle. It can only be observed again by means of empathy.

Empathy lies at the root of the student's capability for true learning, as well as of the teacher's ability to judge the results. And the artistic, playfully-serious teaching techniques tend to release this faculty of empathy. When learning is pursued at this depth, it can meet life successfully, because it is alive within the student; it leads to inner freedom and integrity.

The human spirit would not choose to live on earth if this life were not meaningful to us. And in this world we encounter today the domain of machines, man-made to be sure, but ruled by an order which is essentially foreign to us. We can learn to understand and to control this domain. In fact, only in this context can we grow towards freedom and integrity. In each one of us the human spirit longs and hopes to partake in this growth. This growth is meaningful.

Just as it is possible to nourish the artistic, creative, empathic in the child, so is it also possible to starve these faculties. Turn a child over to all sorts of teaching machines instead of to a human teacher with a heart in the right place, and you will find that gradually such a child will, as it were, turn into a machine himself. He will unlearn to see things in any other way than in a mechanical order.

It is true that computer-based teaching machines, if carried to the extreme which technology permits today, are at present still prohibitively expensive. Consider, for example, the program of the Waterford School, Oakland County, Michigan, under subsidy from the Government Program for Educational Innovation, Title III. The acquisition of machines with the high degree of versatility and flexibility, such as used there, requires a capital outlay of more than a million dollars; operating costs run close to a million dollars annually. But these prohibiting costs are only superficial flaws, which may be overcome in time. My concern is with basic issues of what is desirable, rather than what is within one's budget.*

With regard to judgments concerning the long-range benefit or harm of the machine-world, a child is rather helpless and usually depends on its teachers and parents. In time the direction which these adults provide for such judgments becomes decisive for the question whether a child will live his conscious life essentially at the level of the machine domain—or at a higher level which permits real control of this domain. In order to provide here the right kind of setting for a child, adults should understand and be sensitive to the meaning of technology and its relation to us and to our environment. One should understand the services but also the pollutions and dislocations caused by technology in nature and in ourselves. With every decision to operate a

---

* Skinner's philosophy of teaching purports to provide ideas and methods for the management of education. These ideas and methods do not necessarily imply the use of teaching-machine-hardware and the investment of funds therein. Skinner himself takes a dim view of the effectiveness of the trend towards extensive teaching by means of machines. See, for example, his book: *The Technology of Teaching* (McGraw-Hill, 1968). It is, however, a fact that those who favor — or sell — teaching-machine-hardware take the view that, in so doing, they are implementing Skinner's philosophy: one of the many contradictions which life so often presents.

machine, be it a car, a TV or radio set, or a computer, a feeling of heightened responsibility for one's inner human state should be aroused. This is especially important in regard to decisions to use machines for pure amusement.

If parents and teachers do not hold the reins, the child's empathy tends to be drawn down to the machine level. Raising and maintaining oneself above the world of machines requires, in addition to an *understanding* of the functions of machines, an attitude of *restraint* in their use, a kind of esthetic taste for the conduct of life. Let me elaborate this important point.

Suppose a good dinner is scheduled for six o'clock and the children come home at five. Some can control their appetite; others grab a whole box of cookies and whatever other edibles come within their reach. The latter spoil for themselves the full benefit and enjoyment of the good food when dinnertime comes around. Moreover, they tend to overeat, with consequent damage to their health. Likewise one can ask: Can the need for 'amusement' not be better satisfied in many instances by activities other than the passive stare at the TV screen? Must we ride for our Sunday amusement—could we not drive to a place where one can safely go for a walk in the woods or on the beach?

Parents and teachers face a tremendous responsibility for their children in regard to upholding control of this sort. By their own actions they set the example which will become decisive. A good rule is: *What is worth doing is worth doing well*. And 'well' implies: taking into account the need for balanced activities, which are much more invigorating than the seemingly restful overloading of the senses, just as a well-balanced meal is more nourishing than a pound of sweets.

Never should a child—nor his adult companion—be permitted to indulge in a sloppy, passive, only half-attentive way in technological forms of amusement, such as TV watching or listening to the radio. These acts should be strictly limited in time so as not to exceed the span of really active attention, which rarely exceeds half an hour. During the time of watching or listening no other activity should be pursued; concentrated observation should be insisted upon. The content of what was observed should be made a subject for subsequent conversation, for painting, or for some other personal creative reaction. If one insists on this principle from the start, one will discover that many healthy children require relatively little (but consistent!) coaching, and soon lose interest in these forms of amusement, of themselves, except for some especially appealing programs. Of course, good habits tend to erode in the company of friends who don't have them, and thus they may need reinforcement from time to time. Many other children, however, have already been sufficiently weakened in regard to their inner activity, so that they crave for the trance which mechanical amusement tends to induce. Their continually disturbed motor-sensory balance will gradually turn them into people who lack initiative, are alternately bored or frustrated, and explosively compelled to acts of violence or destruction. They enter on a path of life devoid of deep feelings and deep joys.

That is a high price to pay for the cheap 'amusement' received. The educational philosophy of Rudolf Steiner has a great deal to say about the connections between us and our environment. It is not necessary that all parents become experts in education, and Steiner schools can often clear up questions for parents when they arise. But as a general rule I would like to urge every adult who has responsibility for our generation of children, to do one good deed every day for their sake, by attempting responsible, fully conscious judgment as to when to use the services of technology, and when to restrain their use.

Beneficial control of our overabundant environment can only be achieved through active, sensitive control, from within, of our own inner life.

(1969) —Ernst Katz

Independence In Education

The aim "so to educate children that they will be of themselves able to impart purpose and direction to their lives" was founded by Rudolf Steiner not only upon the what, when and how of teaching, but upon the concept of a school as a free cultural institution. Spiritual freedom is that which allows full expression of conscience, as choices and decisions are made and responsibility for results is borne. A view of educational goals which include the development of capacities of initiative and conscience must also include the ground in which they find root—the school itself. A school in which the teachers are its conscience, and are free to shape the life conditions of the school out of their concern for education, stands as a free institution. Education for freedom evolves to the extent that the ground from which it springs is free. This is what Rudolf Steiner points toward when he shows that "education, lying as it does at the root of all cultural life, must be put under the management of those people who are educating and teaching."

There is no question but that this point of view would be revolutionary to the authorities on school administration in both public and private school systems in America and elsewhere. Yet it deals with and goes deeply into the question of academic freedom which is becoming more acute as political and social problems are intensified by the world situation. It also contributes in a fundamental sense to the question of the future of Western civilization and its stewardship over the free spirit of man.

The extent to which the idea of a faculty administered school is a revolutionary one is apparent when, in the pages and columns on modern education, one tries to find some recognition of the status of teachers as professional persons with a need for self-determination in the practice of their profession. On the whole, the emphasis on freedom presses into the school room, however immature the little community of the class may be; in the adult sphere the teacher, who must nourish the spiritual and moral growth of the children, occupies a position that is far from being self-determining.

The education of children for life in a free world may be complicated by the very effort that is being made to foist the pattern of democracy on children, while at the same time the adults, under whose influence they form their attitudes, depend for their jobs on a school system which is managed by non-teachers. The immaturity of childhood is challenged to exercise self-determination. Those who prepare the challenge are themselves estranged from it. Whether in a public or a private school, the teacher's position is on the lowest rung of a ladder supporting a hierarchy of administrators and supervisors, which in the public school system is intricate and controlled by political means. Even in independent schools there exists the differentiation between administrators and teachers. School administration, a field in itself, is preferred over teaching. The school principal is responsible to trustees who, generally speaking, are not educators. A teacher's professional freedom depends on the personalities who carry the responsibilities for the school as a community institution. In contrast to this picture of what is general practice in the field of education, the notion that it is the teachers who must also carry the responsibility for the school would indeed be radical.

Rudolf Steiner recognized the fact that modern man has evolved a cultural life to a very great degree dependent on state institutions and economic forces, and that the extent to which the individual can contribute from his spiritual resources to the welfare of the community depends on the emancipation of his spiritual-cultural strivings from control by methods which have their proper place only in the political or economic branches of social life. Two of the "Four Freedoms" which have become the gospel of the free world, Freedom of Worship and Freedom of Speech, hint at that which Rudolf Steiner carried further in his consideration of education as an essential part of public spiritual life. He observed that "human beings, growing up to life, are within the spiritual domain of the body-social, and will go forth with views of their own to put into practice". He urged the point of view that with each child there are new abilities growing up and that these will really be passed on into the life of the community when the care of developing them rests entirely with people who can judge and decide on spiritual grounds alone. Because it is the teaching profession which forms the bed-rock in the ground of any educational system, he suggested that the anti-social results of education, which flare up in the individual tragedies as well as the world conflagrations that threaten our age, point back to an anti-social configuration in educational systems, in so far as "the young have been brought up and taught by persons who themselves are made strangers to real life by having their lines of work laid down for them from outside".

"Educators," he said, "need to fix their lines of work themselves, from the smallest things up to the biggest. When they cannot do so, they grow impractical and remote from life. And then you may give them any principle to work on, laid down by apparently the most practical people, and yet their education will not turn out people really practically equipped for life."

In making it clear that the people who determine administrative policies must be at the same time actively engaged in teaching, he centers and unifies the whole field of responsibility within the most reasonable realm of influence. Faced with their immediate problems as teachers, the members of a faculty approach questions of administration from the point of view of pedagogy. The faculty meeting as such emerges as the governing influence in the school. Here is the time, the place and the occasion in which the whole life of the school is centered and from which all progress proceeds. The faculty elects its executive members who are entirely responsible to the faculty. The personal attitudes that may at times interfere with efficient cooperation for the good of the school have to be overcome through individual experience and effort. These are the attitudes, usually taken for granted in less consequential situations, of the prima donna, the agitator, or the one who needs to lean on authority. Each teacher finds that spiritual growth is demanded of him for the sake of the whole. The faculty meeting of a Rudolf Steiner school is the center of its freedom. In this body each teacher is responsible for the whole school. The exercise of freedom is in the adult realm where it belongs. Reflected back, into the classroom, through the teacher's mood and conscience, is the spirit of self-direction which the children look up to as an attainment of adulthood. Through this reality the children grow in the understanding of what it means to become truly social human beings.

In the practice of self-government the teachers in an increasing number of Rudolf Steiner Schools, in Europe, Great Britain and America,* have been tested for more than three decades, and theirs is an essential contribution to the social life of the future.

(1958)   Dorothy Harrer

Linear Thinking

We have no eyes in our back, nor even a nose or an ear. For what is behind us we are blind, and few people have the slightest sense for what goes on behind their back. That is because by its nature our very being shows only *one* direction: forward. There we look, there we go,—even our ear auricles open forward. We are built to be 'hind-sightless,' in the true meaning of the word. How different it is in other creatures: the eyes protrude from the body, they look right and left, they lend circumspection. Consider the fly: how wide is the angle of her sight—nearly nothing escapes her,

* Now for more than seven decades, in every part of the world. See list of Waldorf schools page 210 (Ed.)

except what is below her body! But in people, how wide is the blind spot behind us and above us! In these directions everything escapes our attention.

This attitude of our body is not without influence on our thinking; it aims at the tomorrow,—it aims forward. We want to get on, even to take precautions; at the same time, we want to turn away from disagreeable things: we want to turn our back on them. Certainly, this one-way pointing of human nature has its advantages: we are purposeful; our will and our work have a clear orientation. At the same time, though, we incline to shove aside and forget everything that does not serve the purpose, the goal. A German proverb says: "Where there's planing, chips will fall." Chips—well, they seem to be only trash, but precisely here lies the *psychological* reason for all those problems which by now have grown into an avalanche of waste, to the annihilation of the environment.

We see only half the problem if we merely blame the purposeful and inconsiderate depredation of nature for the environmental catastrophe which now has become a reality. It is true that if we only think of refuse and dirt, the task of healing could be accomplished by reasonable legislation and good will. Why should not the producer of non-returnable containers or of hard-to-destroy plastic articles be forced to a foolproof removal of his products? But we miss the core of the problem if we consider only the environmental catastrophe. Behind that, we find a style of thinking that shows destructive consequences also on other levels. In addition to our one-dimensional thinking we also have a fixation on a limited segment of reality.

Even with reference to vision, it is striking that our attention is clearly focused only on a small section of the totality: we look at one point, one thing, and everything else around that point is blurred. A similar consideration holds for thinking, when it tries to explain the colorful richness of the world by one or two principles. Monomaniac thinking is happy when it has reduced all phenomena to one factor. For instance, many psychoanalysts swear by Mephisto's advice to the student of medicine:

> Learn chiefly how to lead the women; be assured
> That all their "Oh's" and "Ah's," eternal, old,
> So thousandfold,
> Can at a single point be cured.*

Modern psychoanalysts often think that not only women but also men can be explained by one point: sexuality as the only driving force of soul-life! Matter, whatever it may be, as the only basis of all phenomena! Egotism as the only motor force of economic life! And everything else is also "nothing but . . ." Newton has expressed the faith that creates such a style of thought in a moderate form: "Nature, namely, is simple and does not revel in superfluous causes of things."

The idea that nature, truth, and all else is simple contradicts experience; consider merely a forest, a pond, or the human body. They all are organisms, living communities, maintaining their existence in thousandfold relationships in a mobile balance, from microflora to macrocosm. It is a web of interdependencies never to be comprehended by linear or static thinking. The opinion that truth, nature, and man, as well as all else, are simple is based neither on nature nor on truth nor on man. That opinion is the product of a depleted thinking, reduced to a meager line: because of its own desiccation, it cannot grasp the manifold or the multicolored and reduces them therefore to the gray in gray of two or three factors. The monocausal thinking, which monomaniacally aims at unity, is weak, and therefore it seeks support in everything subject to measure, number, and weight. An example: the individual form of human talent is reduced, without consideration for any special characteristics, to an I.Q. This measuring and normalizing of the intelligence can be taken as an example of many instances of measuring: by assignments, taken mostly from school life, or from the

---

* Goethe, *Faust*, Part I, translated by G. M. Priest. Knopf, 1941.

intellectual realm, intelligence is defined—when the very fact of such a definition already is arbitrary. With this, a specialized, trained, easily measurable form of intelligence is declared "*the*" intelligence. One forgets that this specific form is not the fundamental or original one; furthermore, one forgets that there are other, quite different forms of intelligence. Who ever considers the countryman's intelligence used in herding cows, in plowing, in making hay, and in milking? It, too, is an intelligence,—in fact, a practical one. Who considers the esthetic intelligence of an artist composing a picture? Who considers the persuasive skill of a public speaker, or the religious-ethical genius? All these forms of intelligence are ignored.

So far the problem is theoretical. But now imagine that the intelligence tests are used for practical purposes, let us say, to find the best method of instruction. A totally one-sided concept of intelligence then ("intelligence is what the intelligence tests measure") is held up as the yardstick for evaluation. It decides how instruction should be given. In this way, a definite, one-dimensional form of intelligence begins to eternalize itself. The false becomes reality. Whatever is most easily measured is often the least important. Size and weight of an orange tell us nothing about its nutritive value, its vitamin content, or its flavor. The qualitative tends everywhere to escape measurement—and yet the qualitative is the important thing. It can be recognized, however, only by imaginative thought, by experience, and by dealing with reality.

Real experience eludes the one-dimensional thinking that reduces nature and man to what can be measured. In the economic sphere this type of thinking corresponds to the calculations of industry, for which price in numerical dollars and cents is the last instance, the only reality. One does not ask: what kind of product do we really need, but rather, what can be manufactured most cheaply and sold at the highest price? This attitude is especially dangerous in agriculture, which should be really concerned with the care of land and soil, and in education, which can and should awaken free, unregimented individualities. Of course, we can force the earth-soil to yield, quickly and cheaply, large harvests—just as we can quickly teach reading, writing and arithmetic to children. But whether the exploitation of the land does not finally lead to the annihilation of the soil, or the exploitation of the children does not lead to emotional erosion and instability—this cannot be decided by any test, any price calculation; this is, in the last analysis, decided by life itself. Only one who has the patience to observe living results, not today or tomorrow but in twenty or fifty years' time, will be able to experience what quality is. He will find out whether a method of instruction is really educative, whether food is really health-giving. Life itself is the forum before which the truth of thinking must be judged.

(1971) —Christoph Lindenberg

Translated by Ruth Hofrichter, with the kind permission of *DIE DREI, Zeitschrift für Wissenschaft, Kunst und Soziales Leben* (June, 1971).

It's Easy to Start a Waldorf School ... But ...

The growth of Waldorf education in North America—so slow for so long—is now accelerating rapidly. In 1968, some 40 years after the founding of the first school in New York City, there were just eight schools and three of these were infants. The next decade has seen nine more come into being. More significantly, there are almost countless centers where groups of people are thinking or working actively to found new schools.*

The need is great. Even 50 or 100 Waldorf schools on this continent would be all too few to meet the needs of those families that want this education for their children, and to be resource centers for the enlightenment of other teachers. One cannot but feel a great sense of urgency, particularly as the conventional human image darkens under the influence of concepts such as behaviorism, sociobiology and the like, and in turn the public schools, news media and books pick up and deluge us with such soul-destroying doctrines.

But the need is even greater that each and every Waldorf school be strong and be true to Steiner's impulse. A weak school can drain our scant resources, and we have none to spare. A school not really working out of the knowledge given by Steiner, not fully dedicated to the spiritual and cultural renewal implicit in it, cannot truly be a Waldorf school, and its shortcoming will reflect on all other schools and on the good name of the whole movement. Any school which fails, or falls short, will leave a legacy of shattered hopes, even bitterness, which will hamper all the rest.

It's easy, all too easy, to found a school. A teacher, a room or two, a few hopeful parents and their children, glowing words and visions—and you start. But then . . .

---

* Now in 1993 there are—give or take—100 Waldorf schools in North America and four teacher training centers.

Problems arise. Teachers find they face issues and questions new to their experience. Parents query some specifics or are disappointed with their child's progress in reading or don't pay the agreed-on fees. The landlord is uncertain. Faculty openings cannot be filled with trained people, and substitutes don't understand why it must be done just this way. Cash shortages prevent full salaries being paid, and teachers are burdened with personal financial problems. Good co-workers leave. Space, equipment, faculty and funds aren't adequate for next year. Applications dry up. Disagreements arise between good, dedicated people. And suddenly it seems that the school which started so easily cannot survive. These examples are not hypothetical. It can all too easily happen. For while it is easy to start a Waldorf school, it isn't easy to sustain it through its formative years.

Every parent knows what is involved in raising a child through infancy, childhood and adolescence. A school goes through a similar maturation process. A new beginning school should consider quite objectively whether the initiative is sufficiently substantial, or whether in reality it may be a radiant, floating bubble of enthusiasm. No Waldorf grade school should be started without assurance that it will continue.

What, then, should be considered if and when the impulse arises in you and in your circle of friends to start a Waldorf school?

The first step for such an initiative group would be to ask themselves three basic questions:

1. *What really is a Waldorf school?*
2. *Why do we want to start a Waldorf school?*
   What is our motivation?
3. *What does it mean to be responsible*
   for starting such a school?

Superficial observation might suggest that a Waldorf school is a pleasant school where lovely people teach beautiful programs. In fact, any school could use Waldorf techniques and methods and be a very fine school—but still not be a Waldorf school. It becomes one when its teachers are united in a common inner commitment to an image of the spiritual nature of the human being, and live and work out of that commitment. A Waldorf school is an embodiment in a practical way of a spiritual undertaking for spiritual and cultural renewal. The understanding of this task comes from the spiritual science of Rudolf Steiner (also known as anthroposophy). The initiative of beginning a new Waldorf school requires a conscious recognition of this deeper significance and a willingness to accept responsibility for it. Without the spiritual reality coming alive as its center, the potential of a Waldorf school cannot be achieved.

Each school is unique and begins in a different way. The initiative may be set in motion by teachers or parents or anthroposophists, or interested people with a social healing impulse. Someone has been moved by an idea, a vision. The nature of this vision will influence the form and character of the school, and will draw the co-workers together. It could be a city school for deprived children, a country school close to nature, a small school to fulfill the needs of a particular community, a demonstration school contributing to general educational development, and so on. Waldorf schools, because they are based on that which is universally human, are adaptable to any situation, any culture and any social background. In every case, however, an initiative group unites to work together toward an ideal that is greater than any one individual.

Starting a school is a deed which goes far beyond the needs of the personalities of the moment. It is a creative act, setting something in motion which cannot be casually abandoned. One can expect trials and obstacles which test the strength of commitment of the members. Each step is a growing process for the people involved and a test and preparation for the next step.

A thorough understanding of the spiritual foundation of the school need not be a commitment of every person who becomes involved in the practical work, nor of all parents who enroll their children. It must, however, be carried by the responsible members. These 'responsible' persons include the teachers. While each Waldorf school is autonomous and comes into being through free, individual, local initiatives, a group founding a school undertakes a moral responsibility and commitment to ever widening circles affected by their deed.

Getting down to business, how does one go about getting a school started ?

It takes quite some time to prepare the ground and to build up a strong enough center of intensive interest to sustain a school. In most situations out of several hundred initially interested people, a small percentage will be sufficiently motivated to investigate what the school can offer. Of these an equally small percentage will be courageous enough to actually entrust their child's future to a new school. Therefore a broad base of interest and support needs to be built up, forming a pyramid from which only a few carry their interest all the way to the peak. In Toronto where a school was opened in 1968, study of Rudolf Steiner's educational philosophy by small groups of people, including periodic public lectures, had been in progress for some 13 years previously. Regrettably the urgency of this decade does not permit so lengthy a preparation; a school's start would be much stronger and steadier if it could.

Planning for the practical needs of a grade school should be started two to three years before opening. It will be a rare occasion when all the necessities can be adequately prepared spontaneously. This means the group has to 'sense' their situation and envision a realistic target to work towards.

The practical steps could be divided into four basic areas, which should all be in control before opening a school:

    I. *Teachers*
    II. *Children, parents and public*
    III. *Buildings and equipment*
    IV. *Finances*

Much could be said on all these points, but a few brief comments must suffice.

Without the first—the teachers—there can be no school. This matter is therefore of primary importance above all others. In starting a new school it is of immense value to have at least one experienced Waldorf teacher with the kind of depth of understanding of Steiner's philosophy of education attained only by maturity and experience. Due to the rapid expansion of the movement, these persons are all too few and are frequently much needed in their present schools to train young teachers.

It could happen that a school simply must begin and no Waldorf teachers are available. A very good school or kindergarten can be established incorporating as much as possible of Waldorf ideas. Care should then be taken not to misrepresent the facts. Give the school another name; add the name of Waldorf only when it has achieved this goal.

One of the best ways of contacting parents and children is to set up a pre-school program in the same geographical area where you intend to start a grade school. A pre-school program is an extremely valuable service to children, especially in our time when so many destructive influences can impinge on the child in the early formative years. A program up to Kindergarten level can be continued for many years without requiring any commitment to a grade school. It can be carried by a small number of people. Care must be taken, however, not to give in to the inevitable pressure by a few eager parents to start a grade school prematurely. The need is so great and the children so ready! But this situation prevails everywhere. We can only do a very little in the face of great needs; we are still very few people spread very thinly. What we do must be done rightly and solidly.

The image the school projects is an important concern. Every piece of paper, every human contact, every display will be scrutinized by the enquirer as representative of Waldorf education.

A good teacher can educate in a barn or under an oak tree! Nevertheless, because a Waldorf school tries to reflect its philosophical values in every aspect of its work, the outer appearance and environment of a school building are important. Local regulations for schools generally govern such matters as land use, by-law conformity, floor space per child, washroom facilities, parking and transportation accessibility, and fire regulations. The fire regulations are generally the most stringent and may make the conversion of an old house or building prohibitive. Even while accommodating all the necessary regulations, we can become distinctive by greater dimensions of imagination, human warmth and artistic sensitivity in how we use or embellish our facilities. Rudolf Steiner emphasized the long range effect on the developing child of architectural forms and the quality of the environment; he even gave indications for suitable colors for the walls in the different classrooms.

Finances are a very necessary component of life and we must be the masters of the balance here, too. All planning—for faculty, other staff, premises, equipment, supplies, enrollments and fees—can and should be worked down to dollars in and dollars out. Some assumptions and guesses may be necessary at first, but you can obtain through budgeting an idea of net needs in advance. Those people you approach for financial assistance will be more likely to support the project if they see realistic, sound planning and feel that they are being asked to close a financial gap rather than fill a bottomless hole.

It is almost certain that fee income can never do much more than cover operation costs. A new school will likely have a deficit of at least $10,000 per year for the first four years of operation, not including purchase of major equipment. Financial support for this should be guaranteed *before* starting the school. Additional funds for land acquisition, construction or major equipment will have to be raised through gifts or loans. Money that is freely given carries a gesture of support and love, bringing more than tangible benefit to a school.

The teachers carry full responsibility for the totality of a Waldorf school, and this includes finances and administration. But they will need the assistance of staff and advisors, because they must be aware of the ramifications of their decisions and be able to see clearly their school's needs in the basic dollars in and dollars out of budget management.

Starting a Waldorf school is a challenge. It involves learning to work as one of a group; accepting disappointment or hard knocks and remaining steadfast; learning from mistakes; and learning to love what must be done. It requires the patience to wait for the right time to move in harmony with human and spiritual needs; the selflessness to listen to the quest of others; the courage to persevere toward the goal in spite of hindrances and difficulties. There are rewarding surprises when new help appears 'out of nowhere'. There is a revitalizing energy when a group together discovers a new understanding of education or of human potential.

(1978) —Shirley and Bob Routledge

A more complete version of this article, with the title *Infancy of a Waldorf School* by the Routledges, is available from the Association of Waldorf Schools of North America (AWSNA), 3750 Bannister Road, Fair Oaks, CA 95628 ($4).

Waldorf Education and the Public Schools

The editorial of the July 1976 number of CHILD AND MAN states that Dr. Steiner had hoped that the Waldorf School Movement could work as an inspiration to the public educational world and that new ways of thinking and teaching could begin to penetrate the educational establishment. Now there are Waldorf schools all across the world. Yet, to take America as an example, to what extent have these educational ideas at all affected the public school establishment?

As a public school teacher myself, I feel qualified to assert that Steiner's ideas have had no impact on public schools in this country. I think the basic reasons for this are threefold. The first of these reasons is found in the public schools themselves. Many public school teachers, I believe, are not searching for a spiritually deep quality of understanding of children, such as Waldorf education provides. The predominant idea is to teach in a way that gets quick results, not in a way that touches the depth of a child's heart. Also, there are many public school teachers who simply don't bother to think about what the purpose of education actually is. They take the state textbooks, without question, and teach out of a state teacher's manual, without ever using their own discrimination in what to teach or how to teach. And an interest in Waldorf education, after all, would have to develop out of an interest in or true understanding of the purpose of education.

The second and third reasons for the lack of public impact of Steiner's ideas on education stem, I feel, not from the attitudes of public teachers, but rather from the attitude of many Waldorf teachers. I have met several Waldorf teachers who just assume that it is impossible to teach according to Steiner's methods in public schools. They have an image that curriculum and teaching approaches are rigidly dictated by state and local education administrators and that teachers really have no freedom to apply Steiner's ideas in any way at all, even if they wanted to. In a moment I'll examine this premise.

Also, and perhaps most importantly, Waldorf educators tend to have the idea that Steiner's methods should not be employed in public schools unless the entire school can be totally devoted to Waldorf education. In other words, there's an idea that education must be pure—all or nothing, so to speak. If Waldorf methods are going to have any real effect on children they must be systematically employed over the child's entire school career. In addition, some have the attitude: who is going to use Steiner's methods in the public schools? The teachers there have not gone through Waldorf training and they are really not qualified to utilized such methods. And if Waldorf methods are used by untrained people in a haphazard way, what are the children really gaining?

How compelling are these points, and is Waldorf education, therefore, destined to merely serve the needs of a few children in only a very few neighborhoods? Is Dr. Steiner's plan, for the Waldorf impulse to penetrate the entire educational world with new insights, an outdated pipe-dream?

The answer to this question, I think, will depend on the predominant attitude Waldorf teachers have towards this form of education. Many spiritual questions boil down to a matter of one's attitude. Let me illustrate the two main attitudes I have encountered with regard to the present topic: Several years ago while some eurythmists were visiting Berkeley, California, I had an opportunity to attend my first eurythmy workshop. I had been a student of Steiner education for many years and a friend of the local Waldorf schools, but had never had the opportunity to learn eurythmy. I became very enthusiastic about the prospect of trying eurythmy in my public school classroom. But when I spoke to one eurythmist about this, he said that I should not try to teach any eurythmy to children unless I really had some lengthy and qualified training at a eurythmy school. Several months later I was able again to study some eurythmy with a different teacher and I posed the same question. This time I was told that it would be a very significant and important experience for the children in my class to learn a little eurythmy and that I should try to do whatever I feel able to with them. She said, in effect, that some eurythmy taught even by such a novice was better than no eurythmy.

So here are the two points of view, illustrated through this eurythmy question. But the question is, is Waldorf education the exclusive possession only of those who have been formally trained in such things, or can any interested educator learn what he can through books, lectures, visits to Waldorf schools, etc., and try to put those ideas into educational practice in his own way? Obviously, my own bias leads me to accept the latter attitude. In this way, the Waldorf approach can become an important influence in American education.

At this point it may be of interest for this public school educator to share some of his successes with the Waldorf impulse in the public schools. The fact of the matter is that public school teachers have an incredible amount of freedom to teach what they want in the manner in which they feel is best—especially if they can intelligently defend what they're doing to an administrator. There are, of course, some principals who would make it nearly impossible to do much in the way of Steiner approaches. But the majority of administrators I have met believe strongly in the right of teachers to approach lessons in the manner they see fit. In my own case I have worked under two principals who have not only allowed me to use Steiner's ideas but who have become enthusiastic about such approaches and actually encouraged me. My first principal even went so far as to make my class open to children by parent request only, so that those parents who really wanted a more Waldorf approach for their child's education would be sure of getting it.

Basically the key to Waldorf education is the teacher. If the teacher looks at the world in a spiritual way and understands the occult side of developmental psychology and how children learn at various stages of inner and outer growth, then his educational approaches will be automatically transformed, regardless of his knowledge of exact Waldorf curriculum. In my own case, I was a theosophist and later a student of a Sufi school, so that Steiner's spiritual approach to education from the beginning of my career became my inspiration in working with children.

Thus with this motivation, I was able to study enough of Steiner's educational works to really bring about a change in my classroom approaches. I began to save larger blocks of time for formal lessons in the morning, rather than following the typical public school habit of jumping every twenty minutes from one subject to another. I began to have the children do most of their writing on unlined paper, using the crayon technique of shadowing the paper which several Waldorf teachers have shown me. I began each day with some little eurythmy exercises and with the rhythmic reciting of poems and of the various times-tables, sometimes with the children standing still, at other times marching around the room. Also math lessons were approached first through rhythm and then through an artistic method with stories and with the children again shading their papers. I found that the more of these approaches I attempted, the more my intuition would flash me new lessons or approaches for the next day. I would be doing my evening meditation at home and suddenly get a brilliant idea of an imaginative way to approach, say, the grammar lesson for the next day.

One thing that I wanted to do was to find a way to keep children in my class for more than one year (without flunking them). My answer was to design a three year, multigraded class wherein I had ten second graders, ten third graders and ten fourth graders, while the old second and third graders would rotate into the next grade. This multigradeness worked very successfully because I made sure I separated the kids for various lessons so that I could give each age what was needed. For instance, I did a great deal of work (even plays) with only the fourth graders centered around Norse Mythology. Yet the different ages were still in the same room so that they could help each other and share with each other.

This class was so successful that there was always a long waiting list of children whose parents wanted them to get in. I've found that many, many parents who have thought deeply about educational issues really want something offered in the public schools. They are upset about the joyless, boring approaches used in the so-called traditional classrooms, and they are not much more impressed with the undisciplined "open classroom" approach. There are generally very few classrooms operating anywhere between these educational extremes in the public schools.

Many people in the educational system are desperately seeking new answers to the problems of education. Traditional public education teaches the basics all right, but it makes kids either into lifeless automatons or violent rebels of the system. Open education, on the other hand, does foster a certain spirited creativity, but this at the expense of a systematic, enlightened curriculum and a disciplined respect for authority. I really am not sure whether there are many educators who are ready to understand the spiritual foundations of the Waldorf methods, but I do know that there are plenty who are ready for the Waldorf blend of creativity and discipline, joyfulness and structure, and for the inspired combination of feeling, thought and will activity into all curriculum approaches. As I stated at the outset, part of the reason Steiner has not had an impact on the public schools is that there are many teachers who frankly would not be the least interested in Steiner's approaches. But there are many, many others who are not presently interested solely because they have never actually encountered his educational work.

So what can be done to at least give public educators a chance to learn about Waldorf and be exposed to Steiner's impulse? First, let Waldorf teachers lecture and share their ideas with the public and with more university students, with less of the attitude of recruiting new students for Waldorf schools and with more the attitude of changing public consciousness about educational issues. Let Waldorf spokesmen write more and more articles for public teaching journals such as LEARNING magazine, and advertise Steiner's educational books in these same magazines. Finally and most importantly, I think summer workshops and mini-courses in Waldorf approaches, eurythmy or the philosophical base for education (i.e. *Study of Man*) geared for public school educators should be offered. Publicize these summer courses through local school districts, universities and teachers' unions. Teachers are great ones for attending workshops—so Waldorf workshops must be offered; there is little doubt that they would meet with great success.

Unless John Gardner's dream of true educational freedom in America is fully realized, I think it's safe to say that private schools will never meet the needs of the vast majority of parents and children in this country. Therefore let us work for Dr. Steiner's plan of channeling his spirited impulse toward the revitalizing of public education. At the very least something should be done so that educators will at least have heard of Rudolf Steiner. Public education in America is crying out for some sort of reorienting inspiration. Let the Waldorf Movement help provide that inspiration.

(1977) —James Peterson

We must strive to educate in such a way that the intellect, which awakens at puberty, can then find its nourishment in the child's own nature. If during his early school years he has stored up an inner treasure of riches through imitation, through his feeling for authority, and from the pictorial character of what he has been taught, then at puberty these inner riches can be transmuted into intellectual content. He will now be faced with the task of thinking what up to now he has willed and felt, and we must take the very greatest care that this intellectual thinking does not appear too early. For a human being can come to an experience of freedom only if his intellectuality awakens within him of itself; but it must not awaken in poverty of soul.

Rudolf Steiner

II

THE UPPER GRADES OF THE ELEMENTARY SCHOOL

MORNING VERSE

I look into the world
In which the sun is shining,
In which the stars are sparkling,
In which the stones repose,
Where living plants are growing,
Where animals live in feeling,
And human beings, blessed with soul,
Give dwelling to the spirit.

I look into the soul
That lives within my being.
The World Creator weaves
In sun light and in soul light,
In world space there without,
In depths of soul within.

To Thee, Creator Spirit,
I will now turn my heart
To ask that strength and blessing
To learn and work may grow
Within my inmost being.

Rudolf Steiner

(For Waldorf School classes above fourth grade, first thing in the morning.)

A Class As A Community
A Talk to the Parents of the Fifth through Eighth Grades

Some time ago one of our students, who had gone abroad for a year, wrote me that she was with her class and their teacher on a 3-week sojourn in the mountains to learn what it means to live as a community. Her question to me was, "Why can't we do something like that in the Steiner School?" I would not tell tales out of school except to point up the fact that community spirit is hard to come by, for when later we did undertake a 3-day class trip, she was on hand and contributed several yards of paper toweling to wrap around and muffle the rising bell, and it was easy for her to misread the importance of promptness to meals and of not hiking off into the woods without a word to anyone.

Attainment of social consciousness can be a soul-shaking experience for a fourth-grader. The day came when the fourth-graders were to start using fountain pens. It was a great day for them. "These are not toys," said the teacher, explaining their care and use. Each pen became a personal treasure. Each fourth-grader felt exalted by the sensation of writing in ink. Then came another day when at least half of the class admitted that they couldn't find their pens. Now a sense of trouble bore down on everyone. What could have happened? What could be done? The heavy concern burdened the day, from one lesson into the next, far more important than the instruction in arithmetic or English or French—whatever the subject might be. Toward the end of the day the pens were found under a pile of school bags in a dark corner of the closet. Astonishment! Who put them there? Why? No one seemed to know. The class teacher made a flat statement. "Someone in the class did it, and that person is not going to feel happy until he or she has told what he knows, at least to me." The teacher found a boy waiting for her in the classroom before the class arrived the next morning. His eyes were wide with compunction but he said nothing. "Did you hide the fountain pens?" she asked. He nodded. "Did you do it to upset everyone?" He guessed so. The teacher felt relief. "I will tell the class only that the person who hid the pens told me about it. I know that will make everyone feel better." The boy took a breath and said that he wanted to tell them himself. So he did, and after he had spoken to them, there was a great outpouring of good will. "Good for him!" they said, recognizing the courage in his confession.

Education toward community feeling can include more than what happens seemingly of itself in an interacting group. For one thing it can include the experience of *wholeness*. Twenty-four first-graders begin to take it in as they move in a circle to the rhythm of ∪ ∪ —

> "We are all one whole class,
> One by one see us pass
> While our feet sing the song—
> 'Two short steps and one long.'
> Now we walk two by two
> In a ring round and true
> While our feet sing the song—
> 'Two short steps and one long.'"

and so on, dividing into threes, into fours—all parts of the whole class.

As second-graders they can scan a whole number, for instance 24, and discover that it contains a wealth of number tables: 2, 3, 4, 6, 8, 12, as well as itself and 1.

Teaching from the whole to the parts, disclosing their inter-connections or relationships, placing the human being at the heart of a matter, these can be the guiding principles in the forming of the lessons.

Most of you are acquainted with the key subjects of our main lesson curriculum through the first four grades. The fairy tales, fables, legends and Bible stories picture human capacities and deeds. Nature stories, descriptions of animals, man's work in building and farming lead the children into the world around them. In the fourth grade the Norse Myths encompass, through the deeds of the gods, the confrontation of good by that which is evil; and the study of "Man and Animal" is a comparison of the wholeness and freedom of man, in any environment, with the animals who have developed to an extreme some part of their physical organism in relation to a natural habitat.

It isn't my purpose now to present the elementary school curriculum for grades five through eight, but to give you an example of how a teacher might apply the guiding principles I have mentioned to the presentation of a subject.

In springtime, when the plant world is reawakening, the fifth-graders can be introduced to a study of the plants with an imagination:

"From a giant arose heaven and earth:
from his bones the rocks and stones;
from his blood the rivers and seas;
from his flesh the crumbly soil;
from his hair the grass and trees;
the clouds from his thoughts,
the wind from his breath;
and from the heart of the giant arose the Sun.
. . . Even today the giant body of the earth is sustained by the Sun as by a warmth-giving and loving heart." (from Gerbert Grohmann)

More than other beings, the plants are the children of the Sun and of the Earth. Rooted in the earth, reaching toward the sun, cared for by both and by the air and water that lie between, the plants help to unite the sun and the earth, and to provide the right conditions of life for us as human beings, as well as for the animals. Why should we be grateful to the plants? They share with us the food stores that they produce for themselves in their roots and fruits and seeds, and in their stalks and leaves. Mankind gives them care in return for these as well as for other gifts. Neither we nor the plants could live without air and water, but the plants do something that we cannot do. In the process of making food they refresh the air we breathe and release water vapor into the atmosphere to help supply necessary rainfall.

We never see all of a plant at one moment, for some of its parts are not visible when others are; but we can see the whole plant in our mind's eye with all its parts, root, stem, leaf, blossom, fruit and seed.

The "higher" plants are those which are able to develop fully each of these six parts in their proper season with the help of sun and earth and air and water.

The roots, growing downward into the earth and surrounded by its hardening forces, become hard and woody; but the root tips are tender and are the growing part of the root, always reaching further in search of the moisture that clings to particles of soil.

The stem, growing upward toward the sun, surrounded by air, is more tender than the roots because the watery element which the roots drink in rises up as sap through the stem into the leaves.

The leaves breathe in the air and spread out to receive the light. The air and the light combine with the sap in the leaves to provide food for the plant's further growth.

The blossom is a heavenly plant that unfolds in answer to the light and warmth of the sun. The petals are leafy but have color and fragrance and surround stem-like parts that are members of the blossom. These are the stamens, delicate like the petals, which produce the pollen dust as golden as the sun, and the pistil, sturdy and stiff, a continuation of the plant's true stem, in which the seeds are formed. The sap which enters the blossom from the roots is sweetened by the sun's warmth and wells up at the base of the petals as nectar, that lures the honey bees and butterflies who belong to the flowers and to the sunshine and who carry from flower to flower the pollen which helps to form the seeds.

As the summer sun warms the earth, the earth sends the warmth back through the plant as it helps to swell and sweeten the fruit around the seeds. Then when winter comes to nip the fruit, it withers away and the seeds fall to earth to await the coming of spring.

In every seed, however tiny, the plant's whole nature lies concealed within the little seed-jacket which has been hardened by the earth forces to protect the spark of life throughout the cold of winter.

The higher plants develop all their powers in relation to nature's forces in earth, water, air, light and warmth. Human beings develop their full nature in relation to the human powers of thought, of feeling, and of will. When a person does not develop as a whole, he can be described in various ways, depending on what he lacks. We often hear it said of someone, "He never knows his own mind," or "He has no heart," or "He hasn't a will of his own." So, too, there are plants that do not develop all the plant parts. Some lack the power to form fragrant blossoms, others have no leaves, yet others no true roots. These plants have developed only partially what the higher plants have as a whole because they do not have friendly relationships with all of the elements as the higher plants do. These are the "lower" plants. Among them are the mushrooms, the lichens and the mosses.

The mushrooms dislike the sun and grow best in shade and darkness. What should be stem and leaf stays underground with the roots to form a network of fibers, and what we see above ground is a combined blossom-fruit that produces spores that are a combination of pollen and seed.

Lichens love the sun but scorn the earth. They form no real roots, nor stems, nor blossoms, nor seeds. They are mainly the leaf part of the plant world, and they spread by means of little pieces of themselves that separate off and start growing in new places. You find lichens growing on those surfaces of rocks and tree trunks which get the most sunshine.

Mosses love the watery element and are mainly stem and leaf filled with moisture. Their roots are very short and weak, always rotting off to form soil. No blossoms develop, but tiny pods that contain spores.

Other plants that have what approaches an exclusive relationship with one or another of the surrounding elements can be described and observed, such as the grasses, the bulb plants, the conifers or the ferns. The key to understanding them lies in comparing their variations with the completeness or wholeness of the higher plants.

As the fifth grade comes to the end of this study, it takes a look at the earth as a whole in relation to the sun and the plants. An imaginary journey from pole to the equator—through the tundra where plant life is dwarfed because the subsoil is frozen and the sun's force is weak, through the coniferous forests wherein the hardness and woodiness which the earth gives to roots pervade the trees in their needles and cones, and through the temperate zone where sun and earth are productive of the four seasons and the harmonious development of the higher plants, to the equatorial forests where the powerful overhead sun draws the plants up and away from the earth to great heights, even to the roots which can grow in the air, and to the blossoming vines which spread over the roof of the forest like flower gardens—such a journey leads to the picture of the earth's vegetation as one great plant with its roots toward the pole and its blossoms and fruit in the tropics.

In the years that follow on after grade five, when the children by rights disassociate themselves from much that they have taken as a whole heretofore, it is increasingly easy for varying degrees of crises to appear and disrupt their relationships with each other, and with their teachers and parents. Exclusive friendships can become rampant. They can discover disparities between preachment and practice. Their emerging sense of independence appears as self-will. Their burning curiosity can put them in contact with many kinds of excitement. Divisiveness threatens the class community!

The example from out of the botany lessons represents the method that is repeatedly attempted by our teachers in literally every subject throughout the elementary and high school years with the aim of helping the individual child fulfill his nature in relation to the world. Starting with the whole of some matter, what is contained within gives the grand design leading back to the whole which, as the starting point, has become familiar ground. And in the juxtaposition of two kinds of subjects every year, the *humanistic* and the *naturalistic*, a looking inward to what lives in man, a looking outward to the world man lives in, there is little inspiration for self-centeredness, or for detachment from oneself. Rather do the cooperative aspects of life relationships become a cause for wonder and enthusiasm.

It remains to say that when teachers and parents, as an adult community working together for the well-being of a class, surround their children with their interest in the class as a whole, then the class spirit thrives and the community of the class reaches out beyond the classroom walls.

(1967) —Dorothy J. Harrer

How To Present The Drama Of Sound To Twelve-Year-Olds

Put yourselves for a moment in the position of a teacher who must prepare to teach a class in physics. Let us assume that as an introduction to physics he has to acquaint his twelve-year-old boys and girls with acoustics, the world of sound.

He gets out his physics book and from all the pigeon-holes of his memory gathers together what he once learned and experienced at the university concerning the phenomena of sound.

It is really a brilliant sum of knowledge that he has stored away in his head concerning sound waves, vibrating bodies, velocity of sound, reflection and refraction of sound waves, echo, intensity and pitch, the Doppler principle, quality, analysis, propagation of sound, interference and beats!

If the teacher were to be satisfied with this, he would have only to make clear to his children that all sound arises through the vibrations of either a gaseous, watery or solid medium, that the sound is identical with these vibrations and that the whole phenomenon of sound is based upon purely mechanical principles. But now he tries to put himself in the place of these twelve-year-olds, and after some quiet pondering it may seem to him as if a roguish yet earnest little spirit were to pull him by the sleeve and whisper in his ear,—but how is it with music and all the beauty and wonder which it opens up to us? What is left of the human voice, its speech and song, the singing of the birds, the babbling of the brook?

Sound is surely infinitely more than the mathematics and mechanics of vibrations. It tells us something, it is the revelation of something. Do we not recognize by the sound of a piece of metal or wood whether it is hollow or solid, whether the motor of our automobile is running rightly? And yet sound discloses its true being to us only when we look still more thoroughly into its relationship to man. The human being entrusts, through the instrument of his larynx, his deepest and most banal thoughts, his joys and sorrows, hopes and disappointments, in short, all that stirs within his soul to the element of the air. By this means he communicates to other human beings what he wishes to impart to them. Through the element of sound he reveals his own inner being and makes the unheard audible. In the same way the animal presses its well-being or pain through the organ of the larynx and causes the medium of the air to vibrate and to sound.

Does not something sound and sing and speak best within our inmost being? Do we not hear these voices of the silence best when we close our outer ears to the noise of the world? Did not Beethoven write his greatest masterworks after he had become physically deaf?

Yes, sound owes its existence to the fact that something which is inward turns itself outward. It is primarily a message, and the vibrations of the medium are only the bearers, the transmitters of the revelation of an inner reality.

Thus none of the facts in the physics books is either false or unnecessary. But by themselves they do not really represent the whole. They can only instruct us concerning the physical instrumentality. The human body, for instance, also has its existence and meaning only because it is the physical instrument for the soul and spirit. To no other physical phenomenon have we so intimate and close a relationship as to sound. We ourselves are able to produce it, whereas our relationship to outer light and warmth, to magnetism and electricity is only a more indirect and perceptive one.

Through such ideas and considerations the teacher may be able to survey as a whole the subject which he is to teach. The phenomenon of sound then stands before his mind's eye as an actual being with its own special characteristics, behaving according to its own particular nature.

Let us look at the human individuality, for instance. You cannot define its essential nature. But describe some character—how he behaves in certain situations in life, how he acts, reacts, suffers, and so forth, and you have a living picture of his being. This is the technique of the poet when he lets his heroes appear before us in dramas or novels.

The physics teacher seeks, through the experiments which he performs before his pupils, to present the drama of sound, of light, of warmth, magnetism or electricity. He orders and arranges the single scenes into a complete picture and lets the actor and poet, 'Sound', act out his own role. In this way science takes on life. And only what is living speaks to the soul of the child.

So let the scientific expert in the schoolroom not forget that his listeners are twelve- and thirteen-year-old boys and girls full of bubbling life, expectation and awe whom he must help to establish a living, unspoiled relationship to the world, so that they can better understand themselves and their place within nature and the cosmos.

(1953) —Karl Ege

The Chladni Plate — Meeting Point Of Two Worlds

Waldorf students have their first acquaintance with physics in the sixth grade. Worlds of wonder open up: light and dark give birth to sparkling colors that mix in surprising ways (did you know that red and green could make yellow?); a hot-air balloon rises slowly and majestically; a flame dances and quivers, sensitive to sounds we make.

One of the most fascinating experiences in acoustics is the demonstration of Chladni's plate. This is a simple metal plate, usually circular or square, supported in the center. Fine sand or salt is sprinkled on top. The edge is bowed with a violin bow and, with some skill and luck, one can induce the plate to sing a pure note. Behold! The grains of sand suddenly arrange themselves in a sharply defined, symmetrical pattern. With one magic stroke, intricate and beautiful order is created from chaos. The suddenness of this event is a never-ending source of wonder for the children. They hold their breath when the bow is applied to the plate, and then, if the stroke is successful, they respond with a most heartfelt "Aahh!"

A particular Chladni plate can be made to vibrate at dozens of different pitches, each one commanding its own form. The higher the pitch, the more intricate the pattern becomes. By applying dry ice or vibrating piezo-electric crystals to the plate, one can produce notes of very high frequencies, resulting in patterns of astonishing variety, detail, and beauty. The two illustrations show simple patterns on a round and on a square plate. The first form was obtained by bowing the edge, the second one by touching the square plate with a chip of dry ice.

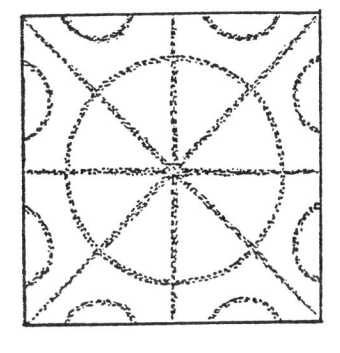

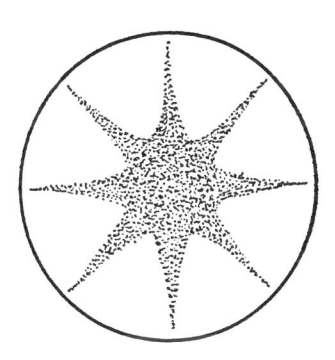

After Chladni's work around 1800, little research was done until recent times. The latest work is connected with the names of Mary Waller, formerly physicist at the London School of Medicine, and Hans Jenny, medical doctor of Dornach, Switzerland. The latter, in cooperation with a photographer, an actor, and a Waldorf teacher, produced a motion picture, "Vibrating World," which was shown on television in Germany and now travels through the U.S.A. as part of an art exhibit sponsored by International Business Machines.

It is hard to describe the fascination of watching the creative moment on a Chladni plate. After the tone dies out, the pattern on the plate remains and can be admired and studied. Yet this is a post-mortem—one is looking at a corpse. The living drama unrolls when the sounding tone, as a dance master, conducts the dancing particles to their places in splendid choreography.

Sometimes one may produce a note with wavering pitch. It is then as if two or more dance masters were giving conflicting orders. There is a struggle between the forms, they change back and forth, and one waits with bated breath to see which will win.

The Chladni plate is a meeting point of two worlds. Material and non-material worlds meet, and it is the not-visible that shapes the visible. Spenser wrote:

> For of the soul the body form doth take;
> For soul is form, and doth the body make.

Emerson said: "Nature is the incarnation of a thought, and turns to a thought again, as ice becomes water and gas. The world is mind precipitated..."

We all experience that a person's face is an expression of, is shaped by, his own unique spirit. The Chladni plate shows that each tone also has its own physiognomy. If a simple, mechanically produced tone has such an intricately beautiful shaping force, the human voice must introduce a still higher order of form-giving. The brand-new invention of "voice-prints", as unique for one individual as his fingerprints, may possibly demonstrate one aspect of this realm. Yet, with all of these phenomena, we are only in the foothills of this landscape. In the background towers the archetype of all shaping forces, as voiced by St. John: "In the beginning of all things was the creative Word..."

(1968) —Gerhard Bedding

The Education Of The Will In The Crafts Lesson

Whoever has had the opportunity of seeing a class of children aged 9 or 10 tackling the task of driving a row of nails into each side of a wooden frame for the purpose of weaving, has had a living experience of that force we call "the will." It is here the still unspoiled, uncurbed will for the working into matter, activity uninhibited by ideas and reflections, the potentiality of the doing whilst the teacher or adult is naturally expected to give the answers to the "What do I do?"—"How do I do it?"—It is an experience that can make you aware in a rare way of the material the child brings to us to be educated, directed and harmonized until it can become activity in thinking, the most human of our human faculties.

When we begin our woodwork classes in the sixth grade there is still much of this blind zeal for the mere doing. Yet modelling lessons throughout the previous year have established a first more conscious contact with matter,—though in the much softer material, clay, and in a purely artistic manner,—and have paved the way for a more observant approach to the material, wood, and its shaping.

The first task that may be given in the woodwork lesson is to make a handle for the first woodworking tool laid into the children's hands: the rasp or file. The word "handle" already lets us discover its close connection with the hand: the hand which is the universal tool given to us by nature and whose working capacity we amplify by the use of a specialized tool. Thus we will study our hand, how it closes up and grips the tool that is made for the specialized job of rasping, and each child tries to shape the handle that fits most comfortably in his own hand when doing the movement of rasping. It is quite a long process, an interchange between shaping by rasp and judging the shape by gripping it with one's hand. The children learn to feel where there ought to be a mould for the palm and a support for the thumb until the square piece of wood is transformed into the tool-holder that gives more scope to the hand. Observation and imagination in the child are called up; the shaping has a purpose and a real connection with the doer. Comparing the rasp-handles in their final shape will then lead to discovering characteristic features which all have in common and some of the work might be called good examples for rasp-handles that everyone would be able to use.

The next tasks are simple utensils such as a dibble and letter-opener. Here the handle grows into a tool. Essential still is the handle,—they are, as it were, prolonged handles. Added to the further exploration of the hand in its movement and grip, the negative form of which can be seen in the handle, are experiences of the qualities of wood as such.

A good way to lead on from there is to extend one's observations of the hand and its functions to the arm, and to study the working process of hand and arm when requested to do the following: There is a tin with cold carpenter's glue that must be stirred. You must stir it in such a way that you reach into the corners of the tin. You have no utensil to do it with at your disposal. What are the movements of your hand and arm when you stir the glue? Observe them carefully, translate them into wood and you will create a really good stirring spoon that serves its purpose. The handle will be slightly curved, the spoon shaped so that it will reach into the corners. In this way the children do not make a wooden spoon according to an abstract idea or picture they carry in their memory, but create something that has been taken from the natural movement of hand and arm. And after some time, according to the children's choice, there will be a variety of spoons: flour spoon, tasting spoon, skimmer, measuring spoon, salad spoon and fork, etc., each revealing its purpose through its form.

The next step leads from the element of movement which can be experienced intimately through the functions of hand and arm, into something that has separated from it, i.e. the bowl. The task here is to find forms which have a direct connection with the two factors: the purpose and the person. Between those two poles stretches the wide field where artistic creativeness can unfold without becoming abstract or purely ornamental. The texture of the wood will inspire a multitude of shapes. The previous work has awakened the understanding for living movement which has now to be metamorphosed into the living gesture. The little bowl that keeps your jewelry over night encloses and guards its content, the fruit or bread bowl offers and encourages you to help yourself to what it contains. Here the actual carving work begins; one works into the wood, carves into it, whilst the previous things were worked on with the rasp and file. Handles and other utensils were shaped by slowly peeling off the raw outside of the lump of wood. Feeling and willing are mainly employed when rasp, file and sandpaper are at work; we feel the form and smoothness of it and the sense of touch is the organ of judgment. This work could almost be done blindfolded. Carving the wood means to be fully awake to direct each movement through observation, to be master of the will power that works into the material and directs its strength at any moment. The working process becomes now a rhythmical interchange of the two poles, will-impulse and observation, and between them weave the creative forces of the feeling life, the feeling for form, which we might call the artistic element.

In the course of the 9th and 10th class the craft lessons become Carpentry. The children are now in the upper school. More freedom is granted and more self-control and responsibility demanded. The task given in the craft lesson is outlined precisely and must be carried out precisely with a variety of tools. Exactitude and discipline of all forces engaged are necessary to understand and make the joints that enable us to assemble parts into a firm whole. Thinking is actively engaged in this kind of work, which has to deal with geometrical forms in the three-dimensional and runs parallel to a main lesson period in technical drawing. A small piece of furniture made by the individual child might result from these carpentry lessons, or a larger piece can be planned and carried out as group-work which would carry the endeavor of an education of the will to laying the foundation for a social willing.

Thus in accordance with the natural development of the child and as one part of the whole of our education the craftwork, too, sets out on a path which enables the child, stage by stage, to get hold of this source of activity and become its master. It is a wonderful power and must neither be suppressed nor broken. But the child must awake to it, recognize it, and the developing mind must set it its tasks, or it will turn into a destructive force. The awakening process engages the child's feeling-life first before the judgment of the eye and clear observation direct the action. The third step demands of the will activity to serve. In carpentry work it has to shed its selfhood and serve the mind and the world of objective laws.

(1960) —Wolfgang Wagner

Reprinted with the kind permission of *The New School Journal*, King's Langley, England.

Wish, Wonder, and Surprise

In seventh grade English lessons, a study is made of the themes Wish, Wonder and Surprise. Rudolf Steiner indicated that these would be important avenues of exploration for young people just reaching adolescence. In teaching seventh-graders, one becomes quickly aware of the richness of their emotional life but also of its chaotic quality. They are up one minute, down the next; they love the world, hate the world; laughter and tears come tumbling out, one after the other. How is the young person to find balance? How is he to learn to find perspective in his dialogues with the world?

The breadth of the Waldorf curriculum tries to meet these problems from many vantage points. This intriguing study of Wish, Wonder and Surprise, I discovered, is one of the most direct ways. We can ponder the three words—wish, wonder, surprise—for many hours. We can ask ourselves as teachers what is really expected of us here. The study goes under the guise of a writing block, so certainly it is a means to study the difference in style between a wish, a statement of wonder, and the description of a surprise. But soon, as one begins with one's students to explore these themes, these attitudes of life, a whole mysterious landscape comes into view.

Wish,—what really is the nature of the wish? Where does it come from? Where does it go to? The wish, we established, comes from within oneself and goes toward the outer world. We began to discover the many kinds of wishes. The most obvious, of course, is the wish for oneself, and here we could begin to distinguish between this and its extreme, desire or greed. Then we could see that one can wish for something for someone else. This could take the more subtle form of a prayer. Further, one can make an impersonal wish that could affect the world at large.

The students dug into the personal wish with gusto. Most of their stories were deviations from the archetypal personal wish expressed in "The Fisherman and his Wife." This theme of man or woman wishing to have more and more power until even God is challenged, repeats itself in most cultures. In the Old Testament stories it appears with Lucifer, who tries to take over God's throne and who finds himself, with St. Michael's help, transformed into the serpent. It appears again in the Tower of Babel, where men's desire for God's power results in the division of the one tongue into many languages, thus making communication more difficult. The theme can be enlarged to include curiosity: the wish for knowledge that is forbidden,—the Fall of Adam and Eve or the legend of Pandora's box. This whole subject of extending wishes into rebellion of authority is very close to the adolescent's heart, and it was interesting to see what terrible endings were the result of this for their heroes.

When we turned to wishes for someone else, the class was confronted with a greater challenge. Now they had to step outside themselves and deal with another realm of experience. There was no gusto in this assignment. The mood was pensive and quiet.

We turned next to surprise. O what a relief! The class found this to be easier, more familiar. Everyone loves a surprise, a mystery. They wrote these with relish and loved a sneaky twist at the end. Where did the surprise come from? Outside—from the world. It came onto or at the person. What a totally different experience from wishing! Whereas the wish streamed out from the heart into the world, expressing a yearning or need, the surprise came from the world and superimposed itself on the person.

The most subtle of the three themes was wonder. When I introduced wonder to the class, it was very hard to distinguish it from a certain element of surprise. The students had to look at it completely differently. They had to distinguish very carefully, had to go through a certain refinement of the emotional life to see if they could experience wonder. Waldorf education is built around the sense of wonder. Surely, from the nursery years on, we try to foster the sense of wonder at the world. But now, in seventh grade, as we consciously examined these emotions, we looked at it as if for the first time. Where did wonder come from? Well, certainly it came from within the human being, but it also came as a meeting with the outside world. Some of the students felt that they could not really feel wonder. We discovered that you can talk about wonder but it is quite another thing to completely feel oneself in an act of wonder. We learned that one has to be open to the world or one could not feel real wonder.

We tried writing compositions about wonder. Some students could bring to birth a real feeling; others were having great difficulty. We left this study, but I was not completely satisfied that we had done enough. We certainly learned that to fully explore wish, wonder and surprise, actually meant to sense the world, the human being, and the meeting of the two. It was in essence to begin to have a feeling for the universe and man's place in it.

After pondering this study for several weeks, I decided to try something more. We took one week, the last week of school. On the first day I told the class something of the lives of Henry David Thoreau and his friends, Emerson, Alcott, Hawthorne, and a bit of the times they lived in and how they met their challenges. The students became caught up in the biographies of these fascinating individuals. In connection with Thoreau's journals kept at Walden Pond, I told them that we were going to do something similar. Every day we were going to go to the bog on our school land, find a spot, and sit silently at that spot for twenty minutes. They could bring no pencils, no paper,—and there had to be absolute silence. Their first reaction was, "How could they possibly sit quietly in one place for twenty minutes?" They were sure they would see everything the first day. I then showed them studies that people had done over a lifetime of one small aspect of the world. There was a collection of hundreds of photographs of different snow crystals.* We looked at them and talked about the subtle differences, about their similarities to geometrical drawings we had done, with plant forms they had studied. Then we looked at a book which delicately treated the subject of water.** We looked at the photographs of water in motion, of the imprint of water on sand, the similarity of the map of water in a delta to a tree and to the lungs of a human being. This recalled our earlier study of physiology, when we studied the development of man and his relationship to nature.

* W. A. Bentley and W. J. Humphreys, *Snow Crystals* (New York: Dover, 1962)
** Theodor Schwenk, *Sensitive Chaos*, trans. by Olive Whicher and Johanna Wrigley (London: Rudolf Steiner Press, 1965)

In order to feel the quality of the journal they were going to keep, I showed them a beautiful book, Gwen Frostig's *For Those Who See*. The delicate drawings of nature, the wispy treatment of ferns and butterflies, the interesting quality of the paper, all of it aroused the enthusiasm of the students. By now they were wondering whether twenty minutes a day at the bog would be enough.

I explained that after we came back from the bog, we would quietly sit down at our desks. On the board would be two short quotations from Thoreau. These were to be written on the left-hand page of the small book each was making. We would discuss these quotations the next day after they had had some time to think about them. On the right side they would write their own observation or thought that had come to them at the bog. They would frame the page with illustrations, leaf prints or designs, so that there would be a continuous feeling throughout the book of what we were experiencing. We would call it *The Book of Nature*.

We left and walked down to the bog. Everyone found a spot and the adventure began. Absorbed young people, sitting on logs, lying under trees or berry bushes, camouflaged in tall grasses, could be seen. At the end of twenty minutes they felt it wasn't enough time, but we adhered to the rules. When we entered the classroom, we discussed Thoreau's statement, "We are what we see." This became the theme for the week.

Day by day the experiences deepened. The young people's conversations changed radically. They became very sensitive to the differences in their spot of bog because of the change in clouds or temperature. They spoke of how much one could observe when one was very quiet. Furthermore they were intrigued by the effort of condensing a thought into a few meaningful words. By the last morning they definitely felt this was only a beginning. Their books were beautifully done, and I as teacher felt that we had really experienced wonder. As a class, we were deeply changed by the experience. A sense of stillness and reverence settled over our otherwise active, bustling group of twenty-five. For a time we felt united in beauty, in awe—an inkling of what Rudolf Steiner might have hinted at when he suggested the study. In contemplating our Waldorf education and him who inspired it, I, too, was overcome with wonder and could only utter a heartfelt thanks.

(1974)   —Betty Kane (Staley)

In Rudolf Steiner's pedagogy the cultivation of artistic capacities plays an important part. If these forces are not developed, or not used, they must of necessity degenerate and lay a foundation for every possible kind of soul disturbance. Through artistic activity, however, the latent powers are absorbed and transformed into positive qualities . . . The peculiar value of eurythmy lies in the fact that the movements are not determined according to an outer anatomical and physiological standpoint, but entirely according to inner impulses of movement arising from the more intimate experience of the forces actively at work in speech. Thus eurythmy is better fitted than any other art to bring the life of the soul into harmony with the body. Rudolf Steiner has often explained that he was able to create eurythmy because he applied Goethe's idea of metamorphosis to speech, and carried the impulse of movement within speech over into the limb-system. It is impossible to explain theoretically in how far eurythmy is an agent for healing forces; but practice over many years has borne this out.

From *Goethe and the Art of Healing*,
by Frederick Husemann, M.D.

First Approach To Mineralogy

In one of his lectures, at the opening of his Waldorf School, Rudolf Steiner told his teachers that the age of twelve is an important turning point in a child's development. We have all noticed that just before and at about the age of puberty, children gradually lose their grace of movement. They become clumsy and crude in the use of their limbs, their manners and even their facial expressions. Their long arms hang awkwardly in sleeves which are always too short. In fact, at this phase of life, we can say a child is actually under the domination of his bony structure, his skeleton. Parallel with this physical phenomenon there awakens within the child a more independent attitude toward his environment and his judgment of parents and teachers becomes more critical

This is the age at which a child should learn the fundamentals of physics and approach, for the first time, abstract arithmetic in algebra. It is also at this time when he is under the influence of his own bony structure, that a child can best learn about the "bony" structure of the earth.

Nature Study in a Rudolf Steiner school begins in the fourth grade with "Man and Animal", and continues in the fifth with botany. During these two years the natural science classes, which always keep man in the center of his natural surroundings, work their way closer and closer to the earth until, in the sixth grade, we reach the study of geology and mineralogy.

Rudolf Steiner advised the widest sort of approach toward the study and understanding of nature as a whole and of minerals in particular. Following his valuable indications we make our start with geography, and in close connection with geographical teaching the children learn to discriminate between a primitive mountain range (granite) and a limestone range. For a class in New York City it seems natural to start with a study of the geological formation of

Manhattan's own granite foundations. The countless subterranean tunnels of the subways and the iron foundations of the highest buildings on earth are only possible because of this solid ground. Even the inner vigor of this city's inhabitants appears to depend upon these layers of granite.

It is important that children should learn and actually grasp the fact that granite originated from the oldest era of our earth's development and is for that reason the firmest and strongest of stone formations. Countless ages ago granite was a vast mass of fiery-fluid substance which cooled slowly while other rocks formed a covering over it. During later ages these overlying rocks were destroyed by water and glaciers until granite appeared as the axes of the highest mountains.

In telling of these slow, majestic changes the teacher should try to arouse a feeling of devotion towards the "oldest altar of the world's creation"—and let the children dwell upon these words of Goethe.

The children draw and paint the stages of the earth's development with pleasure and a sense of discovery. Through poetry, too, a feeling for the earth's wonders and hidden beauties can be brought to the child.

"From placid mountain brow, so solemn, old,
the mysteries of days long fled unfold.
There in time's far-distant dawning morn
the word of worlds in trinity was born.
Its first faint echo, rising from this hour,
bespeaks primeval harmony of power
and strives in white of quartz and dark-hued gneiss
and golden mica like rosin bound in ice
to spread forth pure the altar-table here,
presented long ago to that first year."*

---

* The poems are written by the author, translated by Barbara Betteridge.

The opposite of granite mountains, are the limestone ranges which were created by erosion, as the granite mountains are the products of fiery eruption. Fire and water as the primeval forces in the development of our earth's surface are understood by children without giving them theories. They seem able to grasp how creative and divine forces were at work much as in olden times Vulcan and Neptune were understood when spoken of in connection with the earth's development.

Here is the place for a sketch or diagram of a volcano and the children draw the different layers of the earth's surface descending from sandstone, limestone, coal, devon, gneiss, to granite and the magma, the fiery original foundation of earth.

We soon find out that our whole subject can be divided into four parts: rocks, minerals, metals and gems. Rocks contain many minerals and they in turn are composed of numerous chemical substances which often contain a metal. Minerals and metals can appear on a higher level of development under the special condition of crystallization. Crystals and gems are the rarest and noblest forms of the solid element. And so we lead the children from the description of the rocks and minerals to that of metals and crystals, stressing the point that within these minerals the architectural plan of the earth has become far more spiritual and refined than it is in the crude forms of rocks and of minerals.

As we always try to proceed from the whole to the details, from the original to the descendants, quartz appears as the primeval phenomenon of all mineral substances.

> "As honey held within the white-brown wax
> Was gathered gladly in the day-long task,
> So one day with a hundred thousand suns
> Saw quartz, now hid in mountain-deeps, outspun.
> Beside sun-radiance of quartz appear
> The many other stones but dark and drear.
> For this outshines in age and naturewise

What in the other stones imprisoned lies.
It is the oldest child of light, first-born,
Reminding us how blinded we are grown."

Metals are purified ores. The obvious place to begin this study is with gold, for gold is the archetype of all metals. In teaching about gold we should never neglect to speak of the important part gold has played in all legends, fairy-stories, and myths derived from an age of mankind which we call the Golden Age. Then we speak of the unique qualities of gold in regard to its malleability, ductility, flexibility, its quality of being insoluble. We can beat gold as thin as 1/250,000 of an inch. A piece of gold less than the size of a pinhead can be drawn out into a wire 500 feet long. That is its high ductility. Finally, it never loses its color and splendor: it does not tarnish.

We must always find the threads which lead from the human being to the natural world. When we describe these five qualities of gold which make it the king of all metals, we can draw parallel lines with the five most important qualities inherent in everyone who wants to become a spiritual "king"—that is, a person who knows first of all how to lead himself. Can we not apply these five qualities to our inner and moral self-education in relation to guidance of thoughts, strengthening of will, calmness of emotions, positiveness in judgment and impartiality towards life?* In the Middle Ages there lived people who searched for gold in this way—the true students of spiritual science. They did not want to "make gold" in the superficial sense of the word, but to develop these five "golden" abilities for attaining their "spiritual kingdom". This is the underlying significance of gold in all fairy stories and legends. To the children, of course, the teacher never mentions these facts or comparisons in a literal

---

* See Rudolf Steiner's fundamental writings.

form, but this connection must live as an inner impulse of conviction and enthusiasm within his own mind.

Such a presentation of the subject, including as it does a moral and uplifting undercurrent, prevents a one-sided, materialistic idea about gold and, by indirection, becomes a living force in the child-mind. It reaches the child through the wisdom of a trusted teacher, leaving an impression more lasting than would the mere statement of fact out of a text book.

It is clear that after this the study of silver, copper and iron is easier. We point out that historically gold was the first discovered metal. Silver and copper were used later and iron does not come into use until the first millennium B. C. Iron is the true Roman metal. Lead was discovered still later than iron (about 500 B. C.). We may conclude the study of metals by speaking of one of the very latest, such as radium, in connection with the tremendously mysterious X-rays.

In the final chapter of our mineralogy, we touch upon crystals and gems. Here we look at the greatest works of art which the kingdom of the minerals can produce. Crystals and gems consist of the same elements as the rocks and minerals, but in them the art of building up the earthly element has reached its highest perfection. Crystals have the most amazing geometrical forms, frozen into stone as an eternal law of the world. The ancient Greeks said that "God is a geometrician", and surely crystals and gems are products of this divine geometry. Does it not seem, in precious stones, as though the splendor of the stars had been brought down into the earth itself?

Familiar to most of us is the snowflake—the simplest crystal in the making. The shape of the ice crystal is the hexagonal prism. The Greeks called the ice "kristallos", and from this our word crystal is derived. Starting with the crystals of the quartz-family (rock crystal, amethyst, rose quartz), we go on to the garnets and to the corundum family (pointing to sapphires and rubies, emeralds and topaz) and finally come to the diamond—truest archetype of all crystals and gems.

Diamond is the strongest of all minerals. It can not be cut by another mineral for it is 140 times harder than corundum which stands next in hardness. All other gems consist of two or more chemical substances. The diamond alone contains but one. When pure carbon, or graphite, crystallizes in the form of an octahedron, the greatest miracle of transformation takes place—from the blackest opaque substance to the whitest most transparent one: the diamond. The diamond, then, can symbolize the discrimination between good and evil. We conclude our study of mineralogy by developing moral and idealistic thoughts on this phenomenon. We can see in diamonds the pure splendor of sunlight—as though, in them, the whole earth had begun to turn toward a future in which its darkness will be overcome by the power of light.

Mineralogy brings to a close the study of natural science as given in a Rudolf Steiner school. It is important that we should not terminate such a period of teaching unless we have given to the children a feeling of true veneration for the greatness of nature.

(1942) —Frederick Hiebel

"But Wickedness Has To Be In It Too!"

The children were playing gleefully with some puppets they had received for Christmas. What they played was naturally an echo of past experience. Both 7-year-olds had seen a Punch and Judy show, and both knew the story of the Garden of Eden. From these memories their play was formed. The Devil was an important member of the cast, and since there was no puppet for the part, another figure substituted for him. But soon the tussles with the Devil became loud and vehement. The grown-up nearby, wishing to curtail just this element, suggested that they rehearse more peaceful, pleasant scenes. And then there rang out a cheerful and absolutely carefree chorus: "Oh, but there has to be some wickedness in it, too!"

In the child's second 7 years there begins a perceptive-emotional attempt to come to terms with evil. It is still very much on the surface and not wholly conscious—a meeting on the outside, often accompanied by that good companion, Humor.

In his book, *The Education of the Child*, Rudolf Steiner describes three 'births' of the human being. At different epochs of growth the child liberates himself step by step from enveloping sheaths and gradually forms body, soul and spirit according to his own individuality. First, from the physical body of his mother, which for nine months was a protecting sheath, the child frees his physical body. But his growth- and life-forces are still joined to the protecting sheath of his environment. Through the magic power of imitation he entrusts himself completely to what surrounds him. In this period, up to the age of 7 or thereabouts, he is forming and moulding his body, developing habits, and shaping his memory and thought-processes. At the end of this important epoch, signalled by the change of teeth, the life-force organism is liberated, completely his own. Now the way is opened up to begin to shape the child's soul-organism through his feelings.

Up to about 14, the child is joined to his emotional environment as though it were a cloak or envelope surrounding him. Slowly his own soul-being condenses from the larger whole and becomes an integral part of himself. It is at this decisive time of life—which constitutes, after all, the main part of school time—that all emotional, psychological problems and pre-eminently all the valuable solutions to such problems achieved through the course of human evolution, can be brought to the child in immense pictures. From outside, the seeds are planted which in later years will provide him with the right government of his inner life.

Before he is seven, the problem of evil will not touch the child. Even when he sees the Devil in a play or in a picture—and this should not happen too early—the young child will probably be only amused by the creature's wild jumping or beautiful tail. After fourteen the maturing young person will begin to experience evil as part of his own being, and will therefore keep silent about it; it will become the object of intense and secret inner debate.

Before this, in the happy time from seven on, the child begins to be interested in the dynamics of evil. But it has still the distance of a picture, and does not lie heavy within. At this stage of life the child can still find out how to overcome wickedness, and moreover he has confidence in the wisdom of the grownups around him. So at the beginning, he can shout with merriment and curiosity, "But wickedness has to be in it, too!" He is sure that Punch will triumph over the Devil.

However, before the threshold to adolescence, the child's experience changes. He meets evil, or the possibility of evil, in a totally different sphere: in the realm of natural science. Now the child comes to realize that only the moral attitude of man determines whether inventions and discoveries shall be for the good or for the harm of mankind. In the last few years children have had quite concrete evidence of this,— have had to have it.

Therefore, to the joyous play of the early years, around seven, let us add quite a different kind of proceeding in class, as contrast, at the end of this epoch, shortly before the 14th year. This antithesis suggests the wide range of feelings and sensitiveness to which the child is exposed at this time.

Whatever the facts of science that are given to the child, he will find the entrance to his understanding first of all through his feelings. He will sense, for instance, that light and air are elements related to his own soul-organism. The feelings that agitate his breast are expressed in the flow of air taken in from the outside as breath and given out again. It is the feelings that determine and regulate the breathing and heart-beat.

Light and shadow, too, are not yet separated from his feelings about good and evil. Therefore, before the child frees himself altogether from the soul-sheaths that surround him, we can introduce him—towards the end of the second seven years—to those phenomena of physics that can be taken up by the feelings. Particularly in acoustics and optics can we make a start from the child's soul-world itself and progress gradually towards the objective laws. This is valid and necessary, in order not to harm the child's development through too abrupt or too early an externalization.

A conversation in our Sixth Grade will illustrate this. In such a class there are always a few children who have crossed the threshold of maturity too early. Therefore we can observe clearly the difference in the way of perceiving and understanding before and after the age-change.

First of all in acoustics, with no special explanations, the children are led to experience how an audible tone arises when two objects are struck together. Now, when a whip cuts through the air, there is a whistling sound. Are there two objects, in that case, that strike together? Immediately the question springs up, whether the air is an object. A lively discussion begins. Air can't be an object because we simply can't shovel it together into a heap! Still—the defenders of the 'object' return—we can very well pump it into and out of a tube. "Of course we can," say the others, "but air can't be left to itself. It always needs something or other around it, a boundary or vessel, or else it escapes into space."

Strangely enough, no child hit on the liquefaction of air, even though most of them knew of this possibility. After various pros and cons, a boy finally brought out: "Air can't possibly be an object, for I'm in it altogether, and it goes right through me." Now just this boy showed in other things a certain prematurity and had an acquaintance with much that was not fully suitable for his age. But here in this remark he showed how young he really was. He still experienced the enveloping quality of air. With the conviction, too, with which it was spoken, the remark points distinctly to the part that the soul and also the understanding play at this stage of life. The child's world of feeling is not yet abstracted out of its protecting sheath. The air is sensed as an element closely allied to the life of feeling. The child does not yet separate his own being from the air—it is not yet an 'object' for him.

It seems a long way from the discovery with the puppet theater to the beginning of physics, but it is hurried along in the relatively short space of a few years. An inner thread binds together the two seemingly unrelated happenings. In both, the child illustrates his relationship to a sheltering soul-sheath. Earlier, this shows itself in the complete trust that the child feels in his environment. Later, it is the sensitivity to the natural element of air, that with light seems to stand closest to the feelings (as earth is close to the physical body and water to the growth- and life-forces).

The task of the teacher is not to keep the child sheltered within this soul-sheath, but rather to assist in the process of emancipation and the forming of an individual soul-world within. Towards the end of the second seven years, these steps are taken faster and faster, with ever-increasing consciousness, at moments quite perceptibly. It is in the study of science especially that the child has to develop his capacity for thinking. It is here that he must experience the transformation of soul-dependence into thoughtful knowledge, a change which does not always take place without pain.

It was necessary, for example, after the above-mentioned discussion, for the teacher to bring the children to the realization that air in the physical sense is an object. With this knowledge, however, the child falls inwardly out of his soul-shelter and finds himself in an objective world which exists without any emotional connections. A bond is ripped asunder—and an intellectual interest in the object is awakened.

With the greatest possible care the teacher has to direct these processes, for it is just at this point that the very foundations of human morality are approached. As long as the child feels sheltered and a part of the unity of the world which arises before him in the colorful pictures of stories, he is satisfied by the facts themselves and does not inquire into their purpose. But when he separates himself from the objects and confronts them, there appears not only an intellectual interest but also the curiosity as to what one can do with them all.

A further question will arise. There now will come—precisely in connection with natural science—the question about evil, in a new form: Why do men use scientific knowledge for so much destruction? This is spoken about with reserve and with some anxiety by the children, many of whom are remembering their own experiences (the bombing of Germany, etc. *Ed. note*). Now they no longer can shout, with gleeful conviction, "There has to be some wickedness in it, too!"—but rather, "Oh, if only wickedness were not in it at all!" Can the grownups really be trusted to know that Punch will triumph over the Devil?

Our science teaching is concerned not only with the objective world of matter; a strong moral impulse must be contained in it. Therefore it is important to bring science to the child at a time when it can be taken up by the child's feeling-life,—when it can *still* be taken up by the feeling-life.

The teacher must draw from his own living core for inner certainty in answering questions. Decisive will be the teacher's insight as to the meaning of human evolution and the deed of the Saviour of humanity. For even into the study of science an ethical-Christian impulse can shine. If the teacher can bring this impulse, without a trace of dogma or of his own world-conception into all his teaching material, right up to the sciences, so that it meets the feelings of the child, he will be giving the child an inner support in his soul nature. This support will not save the young person from inevitable inward encounters with evil, but it will be of the greatest help when this occurs.

With this support, the young person with his more and more critical intelligence can now transform his sensitiveness to the meaning of evil into true knowledge. Then he will find direction and strength in his inner development for a courageous coming to grips with the force of wickedness.

(1966) —Georg Starke
(Translated by R. P.)
Reprinted by the kind permission of *Erziehungskunst*, monthly magazine of the Association of Waldorf Schools in Germany.

Children's Quarrels

It is often said that children reveal a great deal of their inner nature through their drawings and paintings. Some time ago, a boy in my class—Wolfgang—provided a picture of himself in one of his drawings that was more convincing than any photograph could have been. It was drawn at the beginning of our study of Man and Animal in the Fourth Grade, when the children were between nine and ten.

At that time the human being was described according to function, as consisting of head, trunk and limbs, in order to show, as we approached zoology, that man—as far as his *form* is concerned—is the focal-point of the animal kingdom.

His head, in which the senses are concentrated, is a sphere. The breast bones are shaped like a basket or barrel, an enclosure. But the limbs are like radiating, branching, out-going rays.

Wolfgang waved his hand vigorously as the children had made these discoveries together.

"I've found something else", he said. "You can see it plainly: what streams into the head at the top radiates out again," and he pointed to his hands and feet.

This was immediately "enlightening" to the other children, and they began to make drawings of it. Wolfgang drew himself in his picture.

After several years and many experiences together, the class reached pre-adolescence and the Seventh Grade. At this time, a very serious division came about in the class. The children had been allowed to build themselves a "den", something that comes up as a necessity at this age. It was in the cellar of one of the boys' houses, and there they carried on their secret club business. Two boys, particularly, were leaders in the class. One was Wolfgang, wild, imaginative, full of ideas and mischief, a natural extrovert of sanguine-choleric temperament. His absolute opposite was John, a very gifted boy, dark, melancholy-choleric, easily hurt, often reserved but with a richly glowing inner life. It was John's parents who had provided the cellar.

In my class diary I find characteristic remarks from both boys. In the Second Grade I had told a kind of fable about sulfur and coal. Sulfur had turned up as a boaster, who then in the course of the story had been pathetically crushed by an earthquake. Modest Coal, however, had been pressed by the great force of the earthquake and transformed into a diamond.

"When people talk too much," I told them at the end, "we get to be like Sulfur. It goes to our heads and then we can be called 'hotheads'. And there is," I added very slowly, "just such a 'hothead' in this class."

Wolfgang, who was the one I meant, wagged his head around, looking at everyone else in the class. "Which one is the hothead, I'd like to know!" he shouted.

In the Sixth Grade, John had read Felix Dahn's *Struggle for Rome* with great enthusiasm. "My favorite story is about the defeat of the Goths," he told me, "and the hero I love the best is that brave, dark-haired Teia."

And now in the Seventh Grade, the children were often in their den, and it was over this club room that their quarrels arose. Some of them suddenly found the place "not good enough" and they began to make fun of it. This was for John a personal insult, and so the first battle came about. After that, John and those in the class who took his side no longer allowed the others to enter the den, and these others missed the games there badly.

For four weeks there was a complete state of war. It made itself felt in all the lessons and recess-times, but one could do nothing about it. If there were no battles at school, they were raging on the street or in front of the cellar. John's parents—his father was a professor in the Academy of Art—very wisely took no part in the affair. Wolfgang was the active, passionate attacker; John ever more doggedly held the defense.

Everyone who has to do with young people knows that such quarrels *have* to arise at this age. If the fights had not been provoked in one way, they would have come about in another, and probably with the same two groups taking sides. In such a situation to try to do anything with moral admonitions would be like trying to put out a fire with them. Volcanoes are there and have to burst forth in order to become quiet; otherwise they will continue to rumble beneath the surface. The dramatic knot has to be fully played out. Words cannot help at all. But an objective, strong, true picture can bring alleviation.

At this time we were studying European geography. With Germany as the center, the East and the West had been treated, and now came the contrast of North and South, as exemplified by the Scandinavian countries and Italy.

The hot, white chalk cliffs of Italy and Dalmatia with their intricate shapes and forms were described, and then the nature of limestone in particular. Limestone soaks up water. On the inside, it forms itself to stalagtites in caves of fantastic beauty. Outside, on higher ground, the land is dry and arid. But in a chalk soil, created by the prehistoric ocean and its myriad living creatures, there flourish especially sumptuous plants: orchids, wisteria, acacia and many other varieties. In this hot country there are active volcanoes and it has to do with this that the chief source of phosphorus in Europe is at Girgenti in Sicily. I showed them phosphorus with its light-filled, golden yellow crystals, and demonstrated how easily it burns and how the stone dissolves into smoke.

The Italians living in this land, who are outwardly of dark complexion, actually have phosphorus-like natures: they are fiery and easily excited. They accompany their words with a rich variety of gestures. Art has been their special contribution, particularly in painting and architecture.

The very opposite of all of this is found in the Scandinavian countries, with their granite and age-old earth. Majestic, calmly layered are the forms of the northern mountains, mightier in their silent monotony than the jagged points of limestone ranges. In the North is little blossoming flora; instead, many tiny spore-plants, ferns and moss in pine-woods and heath. Granite does not let water through, and everywhere there are springs and brooks, called "Elves" in Sweden. The earth is steeped in moisture and in connection with the granite, one finds the presence of metal ores. The south of Italy is the chief source of phosphorus in Europe; here in the lonely North is the largest source of iron, at the Iron Mountain near Kiruna in Sweden.

Farmers and hunters in northern Sweden and fishermen in Norway are, like their landscape, big, calm and silent. A girl wrote about this in her composition book: An Italian often speaks *with* hand and foot, but the few words the Scandinavian says *have* hand and foot; they are handfast.

These peoples are not so famous for their sculpture as for their poets and thinkers. It is in the North that the great sagas and epics have been handed on the longest, the *Edda* in Iceland and the *Kalevala* in Finland.

By describing these two different landscapes as sources of phosphorus and iron, I wanted to appeal to the two contrasting groups in the class, without mentioning them, of course.

And now came a third mineral substance to the light-filled phosphorus and the dark iron: pyrite, which takes such beautiful crystalline forms, and which shines so brightly that ignorant people sometimes think it must be gold.

"Here you can see the finest of all," I told the children. "In this mineral, pyrite or sulfur-iron, the two mighty opposites have joined forces. Iron contributes its heaviness and strength; phosphorus gives its radiance ... The world would be far less beautiful if there were not such contrasts in it, as phosphorus and iron. But the greatest and most wonderful thing on earth is when opposites join hands to form something new."

John wrote at that time a particularly good essay about granite and the Iron Mountain. The picture had brought him serenity, and the whole class gave him respectful acclaim for his achievement. Here in such efforts one can observe how education has united itself with ordinary learning.

I visited John's mother on the next afternoon and heard loud, cheerful noises coming up from the cellar.

"They are all friends again," said the mother happily.

After most of the children had gone home, I went down to the den in the cellar and found John and Wolfgang there with a few others. I was told that in recess-time at school that day, Wolfgang had said very loudly so that everyone could hear, "John's club room is *really* fine!"

"And then we celebrated with a war dance," said Wolfgang gleefully.

There slumbers in every class some sort of drama, waiting to awaken and come to life. But intellectual learning is a kind of narcotic: it benumbs the children. Artistic learning is more strenuous. When the underlying drama is aroused, all sorts of dramatic things take place, including even battles. At no other time, however, has the teacher a better chance to take part actively, in order to build up moral forces, to forge character in her children.

In every family, too, some kind of drama slumbers among sisters and brothers, and we parents must let it find its way to the surface. But it requires our help and understanding; then the tensions can be allowed to reach their end by means of a truly curative process.

(1961) —Elisabeth Klein
(Translated by Ruth Pusch)
The article is reprinted with the kind permission of "Die Kommenden".

Every stage of life brings forth from the depths of human nature the predisposition for definite soul forces. If these soul forces are not cultivated at the appropriate age, they cannot later be truly cultivated at all: they will then atrophy.

Rudolf Steiner

The Challenge of Grades 7, 8 and 9 With Special Reference to History of Art

A speech given in Detroit at the June 1978 Conference of the Association of Waldorf Schools in North America.

I

It is important that we take the time to consider the 7th, 8th, and 9th grades. For some teachers these grades may be called the formidable years—there is so much unknown and undeveloped in the life of the children during these three years. It is like entering a dark tunnel and wondering how long it will be until one sees the light. One of the special satisfactions in having a complete twelve-grade Waldorf school is seeing the students emerge into the 10th, 11th, and 12th grades in the fullness of youth.

We know that the physical birth of the child is only one of several incisive moments—one could say, one of several births—which the human being experiences in life. In or around the 7th year of life, the forces that have been organizing and forming the physical body (Rudolf Steiner calls them the formative life forces, or, taken altogether, the life body of man) complete their initial task and are released now for inner work, as basis for thought and memory. This aspect of the child continues to develop in the period between seven and fourteen (more or less), characterizing what A. C. Harwood refers to as the "heart of childhood."* However, when the child reaches the 6th grade he enters a transitional period of change—the eleventh, twelfth and thirteenth years. The awe inherent in childhood passes, rhythmic memory fades, and with it the original sense of wonder also recedes. This is the dawn of powerful new physiological and psychological forces—Steiner speaks of the impending birth of the

---

* *A. C. Harwood, *The Recovery of Man in Childhood*, Chapter VIII (London, Hodder & Stoughton 1958)

"sentient body"—as the child approaches puberty. With this dawning he is cast into a never-never land, losing the security of childhood and not yet familiar with the new change in the life of feeling he now bears. He feels new emotions, a surge of energy, a sense of self. This often leads to a challenge of authority in the form previously experienced. The child is descending further into earth and a sense of ideal conduct often yields to "pragmatic" impulses and bumptiousness. The curriculum in the Waldorf School reflects this experience of gravity and materializing descent with the study of Roman civilization in the 6th grade. One can sense that the children are experiencing both the civic self-affirmation and heroic strength of the Roman citizen, and the morass in the later decadence of Rome with its gross materialism.

But this is only a picture of the symptoms of change—it is not the essence of the child's being as it struggles to find itself in this transitional situation. The task in the 7th, 8th and 9th grades is not to lose the students in the morass, but to help them rediscover wonder and reverence on a new plane out of themselves. The teacher, and indeed the parent too, must form a shield against which the students push and strike, thus strengthening their own ego by butting up against form and authority. They need to be listened to and sympathized with, and they need challenges to sink their teeth into. Without checks and guidance, they may well become self-serving, indulgent, cynical. An image that can shed light on this phase of life is Dürer's *Christian Knight*, also known as *Knight, Death and Devil*. There one sees the knight moving straight ahead as he rides forward on his horse, the devil holding the hourglass trying to stop him, the skulls and demons leering at him . . . Images of this kind can be helpful to those working with young adolescents.

In the 7th grade there is a wonderful opportunity for reorientation during the Renaissance History block. Here the student can experience great figures who were resolved to see for themselves, do for themselves, and not trust authority for its own sake. There is also an earthiness, a lustiness that we can experience in Renaissance times that is reminiscent of our adolescent students. Just read the street scenes in *Romeo and Juliet* or the jokes Shakespeare places in his plays: the times are bawdy, somewhat crude, in a way that is sometimes embarrassing. Another aspect of the 7th grade curriculum is physiology—which offers a chance to evoke wonder at the beauty and intricacy of the human body, at the relationship of one part to another, at the unity of the whole. This is a subject very close to home, of great interest, and very healing if it is kept objective. There must be a real possibility of vicarious affirmation of the self and of calling forth ideals in a free way, without being dogmatic or preaching sermons to the young person who is enjoying the revolt, with all its inconsistencies.

The 8th-grader is a bit further along in the process. There is a strong feeling of needing or seeking a challenge. He wants his class teacher, and yet he also wants new people. Perhaps he doesn't really know what he wants. He is often unsettled, raucous, having trouble handling the newness of it all. But he wants to feel part of the educational process, not the recipient of prescribed plans; to feel what he is capable of, and what his limits are. He has a certain awe of the high school, of the higher level of drama, crafts, art and music ahead of him. He should itch to try these things in a new way. Interesting projects should be presented, ones that involve a certain amount of curiosity and also a certain optimism and ideal, the promise of things to come, of capacities to be unfolded. It is also a good time for projects that demand working together, and that demand form (a terrible struggle!) as well as involving ideals for the future.

At last the student enters the 9th grade—his first high school year in our schools. The knowledge that the expectations will be greater is there, as well as the need for reassurance. Here the teacher can be very supportive, very helpful in establishing a new attitude. The 9th grade teachers have a wonderful opportunity that does not present itself again in the same way. They can show the way things are expected to go in the high school, set new standards; and because it is all so new there is a certain freshness, a grown-up quality about it that engages the student rather than puts him off. It is a chance to stress order and carefulness in a new way. But the teacher must have the utmost patience and caring, and not ride roughshod over the student's sensitivity.

It is indeed a time during which the teacher has a very difficult task. The adolescent experiences a seething of new emotions. Something new is being born in him, an emotional life whose origin may be quite other than it seems, and which must learn to be comfortable in the sense world. Through leading the students into the practical world on the one hand, and upwards into the world of ideals on the other, the teacher allows the student to unfold an inner freedom—the ability to stand centered and comfortable in both aspects, as he or she prepares for the emerging strength of a free, responsible individuality. Without this help it is more possible for the student to become trapped in materialism or seek escape in eroticism. It is a common symptom of this age to develop egotism and the will to overpower others, to dominate. During this time it is meaningful to begin to talk about the history of consciousness and the struggles through which humanity has passed in its development.

During this school year the students, in their curriculum, study and work with the physical world. They are reintroduced to the wonder and beauty of it, of the machines that are used and the means of communications (in physics), of the excitement of revolutions and change (in history), of the power of thought to take hold of this world (in mathematics) ... They are given an opportunity to come to grips with the problems of our times, stirring hopes and interest in them; to appreciate the troubles, the hard tasks ahead; to feel summoned to courage. These are all important calls and challenges to their powers. But through it all the teacher must be there, appealing to the students' understanding of the long road they are walking with their guides at their side. It is we who will help them, with deserved praise and support, giving them the means by which they will help themselves, and building trust in one another. All through, the teacher has to lay the groundwork of clear expectations and, above all, keep alive the image of the higher self of each young person. Furthermore, we should let them know that other stages of life have difficulties also. This is important to them. So much stress has been placed on the difficulties of adolescence as if after that it is simply full steam ahead. The adolescent can easily become cynical when he sees adults dealing with a welter of problems, whether poorly or well, in spite of their maturity. But a certain kinship between young and old can be established when there is understanding that challenges come to meet us all through life and that there are other critical periods of change. So often the young people's parents themselves are of the age that is fraught with inner difficulties. An awareness of this can help the students to be a bit more understanding of their parents.

It is very important to have time with the class, to consider items of mutual interest, to have general discussion, to help them learn how to handle difficult situations, how to disagree and get their point across in a way that will be appreciated, how to get change without destroying all that has gone before. This will also lead to discussions on government and changes in society.

Dealing with the untamed emotional world of the adolescent can be very frightening to teachers, because it entails the possibility of evil, sin and decadence. It means facing a being in ourselves which we are often loath to acknowledge. What are the negative characteristics of the young adolescent that so often put us off? They include the gross extremes of behavior, the sick humor, the relishing of the dark and seamy side of life. Our difficult task, as teachers, is to remain aware of the higher self in the students while a part of us experiences with them the dark forces that tug at them. Our own ego, tempered by constant striving, will work upon the child's world of passions and emotions in a good way. Working out of our own center, we have to understand the pulls from two extremes. We have to be of this world without getting stuck in it. It is a time of unsubtle experimentation for the adolescent. The students are not sophisticated (at least, not to the extent they think), and one can still work with them. One has to keep their energies channeled. Some examples of activity for them could be: planning field trips, fundraising projects, service projects. Staying with form is very important—they so quickly want to jump from idea to reality without going through form!

II

The 9th grade is a rounding out of the uncertain times, of the time of the feeling of walking in the marsh. The ground becomes more firm after this period—if the foundation is laid on which the next three years can be firmly based.

A central opportunity towards this presents itself in the 9th grade Waldorf curriculum during the History of Art course. Here, all past experience of man can be recapitulated. One can speak of ancient man who opened himself to the universe, who lived, as it were, in a state of spiritual union with it. At least, one can do this if one has first broken through to the realization that primitive man was not a mere barbarian! In cave paintings one can see human beings expressing a special connection with the animal of the hunt, to see the relationship of the painting of the arrows with "the taking of the animal's spirit." Later, as one begins to describe the lives of the individual artists, their development, apprenticeship and struggles, it is important to present an objective picture of all they have experienced, with the tragedies and comedies that are part of life. Here one can reconnect with the childhood forces of expectation, hopes, joys, relationships. The feeling life is stirred as it once was in the lower grades—sadness, gladness, reverence, contempt, the whole gamut of soul life is experienced and felt. Through experiences gained from concentrating on the great art works, including imaginative poetry, out of the forces of the succeeding cultures, and by experiencing music, one can refine and temper the irruptive emotional life of the adolescent.

This brings out for us the importance of art and music in these years. An old quotation reads, "Music alone, with sudden charms, can bind the wand'ring sense and calm the troubled mind." Art and music can act as a salve, a healer of dissonance in the soul; they can bring a balance so that the polarization of emotions is not too extreme.

Rudolf Steiner wrote a verse to accompany the History of Art course:

On a primeval day
the Spirit of the Earth
approached the Spirit of the Heavens,
pleading thus:
"One thing I know
and that is how to speak
out of the human spirit.
But now I beg to learn that other speech
whereby the great World Heart
can speak to human hearts."
The Spirit of the Heavens then, in mercy,
bestowed upon the pleading Spirit of the Earth
the Arts.

One could say that the child in the 7th and 8th grade is like the pleading Spirit of the Earth—cut off from his origins, yearning for the connection with his spiritual home. The Arts are the means by which we find the connection out of spiritual sources and lift the soul out of density and gravity into the light-filled, soothing balm of beauty.

But the soul must go through the experience of loncliness. We help the student pass through it by working artistically with black and white. This also strengthens the individuality, as the adolescent sees so many aspects of life in polarities. We must show through images how to deal with imbalance, not only through art, but, say, in history also. The French Revolution provides an excellent example of a time of extremes, how all the best ideas in the world—liberty, equality and fraternity—could go astray due to excess. These are important considerations for our young people so volcanic in their demands.

In History of Art especially we can reconnect the student with his origins. Art came out of a spiritual connection with priests, magic, ritual and religion. This can be presented in an objective way. In Egypt we can relive what the students had experienced in 5th grade—the unity of priest, king and judge, and the importance given to death and the afterworld. Here there was prescribed order; form was fixed. In Greece everything begins to flow into movement; the life forces are released and literally spill out into the first real smile in sculpture, in a new sense of balance, in the artistic flow of drapery, in the ideal figure. In Rome (a recapitulation of Grade 6) the students can see the busts—sculptures of heads with strong personal expression—sorrow, joy, gluttony, determination—a real study of the individual living in the body. And here, where man had lost his connection with his spirit, we have statues of men impersonating gods.

With the birth of Christ a new experience comes to humanity which had to find its own unique form of expression—at first in symbols so simple that they could be scratched on a wall. Experience has become inward now, as it does for the adolescent; life has its secrets, its catacombs. One can objectively involve the students in the life of Christ through the study of art. With Medieval art, for instance, we have the great working of communities in common prayer to create cathedrals, stained glass windows, books and illuminated manuscripts. This feeds the students' yearning for order, stability, and devotion.

With the Renaissance comes the recapitulation of the 7th grade, with the struggle for perspective, for reality. In the South, in Italy, there is veneration of beauty, devotion and balance. In Northern Europe the people dealt much more with inner life—the shadow, the lower nature. Sin and evil were portrayed in paintings. We see hypocrisy portrayed by Bosch in *The Garden of Earthly Delights* and in *The Miser*. Guilt and excess are shown in Breughel's work as he laughed at man's weaknesses. Grünewald showed the ugly and the beautiful in his most grotesque of crucifixions and most sublime of resurrections. Dürer's woodcuts, with their beauty of detail, appeal in a special way to the interest of the ninth grader. In Rembrandt, with his stress on the inner light of the individual, we approach the student's deeper soul life. We trace in Rembrandt's own life the light that comes from without, from the window, as it were, to the light emerging from within the self; just as the 9th grade student has come from a time of outer authority and develops to a time of inner authority. Rembrandt also shows how everyone is part of a holy family, and he represents the beauty of old people, the beauty of their life experience printed on their faces.

In a brief review of the subsequent history of painting, we show the 9th graders the landscape artists, the Impressionists and the Expressionists, and the Moderns—a glimpse of what should follow in the coming three grades of high school.

Through this course the student has experienced a panorama of civilization—and of his developing self. One has been able to show ideals in life, has given the student a basis from which to speak about them; one has shown a way through the tunnel. With objectivity and precision, one has worked on training the senses. Through the power of art one has healed and brought aesthetics into life, developed in fact an aesthetic and harmonizing sense.

As a special image of what one is aiming for, we can consider Ghirlandaio's painting of *The Old Man and the Child*. Here is portrayed an old man with an ugly nose. The young child is looking up, so lovingly and wondrously. Does the young child see the ugliness in the physical being and turn away, or does the child see the beauty in the soul shining through the old man's eyes? The adolescent is like the young child. Can we help the young person to see the beauty that lives within although there may be ugliness outside? Can he

113

experience gratitude for that beauty? Herein is contained one of the aims in Waldorf education.

And thus, cooperating with the healing forces in the arts, the student lives through the history of poetry, the history of music, and the history of architecture in succeeding grades after the ninth. In each case one is able to refine an element of the human soul and help to bring health to the unfolding human being. Let the artist speak the closing words:

> Flower in the crannied wall
> I pluck you out of the crannies
> I hold you here, root and all in my hand,
> Little flower—but if I could understand
> What you are, root and all, and all in all
> I should know what God and man is.
>
> (Tennyson)

(1978)   Betty Kane (Staley)

Rudolf Steiner, to an artist at the beginning of the century: *"If a genuine color experience is no longer cultivated in our time, and if the mechanistic theories of the nature of color are spread much further among us, children will be born into the world unable to perceive color. Through color, life itself is revealed. But human beings will no longer have the faculty to see the elemental spirits weaving in nature. The world will be gray."*

III
THE HIGH SCHOOL

In its very nature Steiner's educational philosophy stands in the center of one of the great questions of modern education, the mutual relation of the Sciences and the Arts...The tension between the two worlds shifts its ground but remains unresolved. It can only be properly released when a disciplined artistic perception becomes part of the method of natural science, and when the healthy objectivity of the Sciences penetrates those finer feelings on which the life of the Humanities finally rests. Such a marriage of the Arts and Sciences, a marriage in the core of their being, based on the ultimate unity of human experience, is one of the great essential themes of a Steiner education.

> A.C. Harwood, *The Renewal of Man in Childhood.*

Modern Physics in the Waldorf High School

As a science teacher in the high school grades of a Waldorf school I have sometimes heard worried expressions of concern for, or even outright challenge to, the high school science curriculum. Parents often entrust the growing child to the elementary school out of appreciation for the life-affirming, reverent, *inner* quality of the education. But when their children are of high school age they feel it is time for the so-called "real" world. They cannot conceive that a science curriculum within a school dedicated to the meaningfulness of all existence could be truly modern.

Yet Waldorf education had its inception during one of the great revolutions in human thought when the so-called modern physics based on relativity theory and quantum mechanics replaced the classical physics of Newton as the fundamental physical theory. Newton's theory, which was the basis of Western science since its inception in the seventeenth century, viewed the universe in terms of mechanical cause and effect, as if it were a machine. In a sense, the end to this view of the universe as a sort of clockwork, alien to the inmost self-experience of man, was a prerequisite for Waldorf education.

Only within a science that recognizes the validity of man's participation in world phenomena is there the potential for overcoming the feeling of alienation, of being cut off from the world, that has its roots in a presumed dichotomy between observer and observed. Modern quantum physics is just such a physics—although the appreciation of this potential is only just beginning to be recognized. As such, in the high school science lessons modern physics is wholeheartedly engaged.

One aspect of studying the physics of this century is that when done in an epistemologically sound way the distinction between the phenomena we perceive through our senses and the concepts that we use to explain these phenomena is unmistakable. This is true of modern physics since, in contrast to classical physics, the explanations are in terms of quantities that are impossible to experience directly. We can conceive an atom in thought; we can never see it. Understanding the distinction between what we perceive and what we think about what we perceive is extremely important because it is fundamental to all knowledge.

The starting point of a Waldorf science block is always sense experience. In the eleventh grade physics block, for example, phenomena that led men to think the concepts of atomic physics are produced in the laboratory. These are experiences of light that occur in the partial vacuum of a gas discharge tube. I am still filled with awe at the ethereal beauty of the colored light that glows in these vacuum tubes. And, invariably, so are the students. Only after observations are carefully made, as well as feelings awakened, are explanations attempted. And then meticulous care is taken to bring the *process* of constructing a scientific explanation under scrutiny, as well as learning the details of the explanation itself. In this way an abstract metaphysical entity, such as an electron, is seen for what it is *and* what it is not. It is not confused with sensible reality.

Perhaps this can be made clearer if we think about crystal-clear, dancing, cooling, wetting, bubbling, thirst-quenching water. How much of water is explained by *picturing* it as a molecule made up of one atom of oxygen and two of hydrogen arrayed at an angle of 108 degrees relative to each other? This picture is a powerful response to utilitarian questions. We know better thereby how to manipulate the substance, but are far from knowing what it is. D. H. Lawrence put it this way:

"Water is H_2O, hydrogen two parts, oxygen one, but there is a third thing that makes it water and nobody knows what it is."

Anyone can understand the workings of a machine who has a mind to do so. We know their principles experientially through the fact of our having bones and limbs! The so-called "laws" of classical physics used to design machines are often simply mathematical descriptions of that which we personally experience.

This is not true of the technological products of modern physics. We can learn to operate transistor radios, and calculators or computers, but the laws used to explain why they work are not in terms of quantities that can be known through the senses. A physics course in a Waldorf school encourages the students to gain awareness of the status of these abstract quantities, of how they are known through thought, and of what inspires man to think these thoughts. A more ultimate aim—the development of a science that can "read" the operative ideas inherent in a well-ordered world of phenomena (well ordered by thoughtful experiment and observation)—still awaits new conquests of the human mind.

As is true for Waldorf pedagogy in general, the direct human sense experience of the physical world is nurtured in the modern physics course. Many inner questions arise as a consequence of such experience. Contemporary science is a response limited to those questions that further technological manipulations of nature. Waldorf students are, we hope, left open to the deeper riddles of nature as well.

(1978) —Stephen Edelglass

The Human Skull
A Lesson with Grade 10

To-day let us think especially about the human skull.

We have already considered the head in relation to the organism as a whole. We have seen how different it is structurally from the limbs; how it is raised into a position of comparative freedom from the rest of the organism; how it is more or less self-enclosed; how it is receptive in character, receiving through the portals of the senses impressions from the world around; how everything that streams towards it is brought to rest within it, so that, from within the silence of the head, there arise the answering thoughts.

Yet, though the head, in relation to the whole organism, represents one pole of human life and expression, viewed alone, it is remarkably complete. You may, perhaps, have seen, either in a picture or in sculpture, a headless human figure. However expressive the pose of the body or the silent gestures of the limbs, such a figure leaves one with a sense of disappointment and regret—we want the *whole* man. Yet it is quite common to see pictures or busts of the human head alone, and there is not the same feeling at all of missing the rest of the body.

Looking at a bust of Beethoven, we may commune with it and feel that we have before us all that the heart desires. Leonardo's Head of Christ is wonderfully perfect and complete.

Why is this? It is because in the human countenance we have indeed before us a whole man: thought, feeling, and will are all there, and in the balance of these three, in the detailed cast of feature, in the animation or dullness that pervades the face, in the lightness or fixity of expression, something of the underlying character shines through to us,—we behold and we know the man.

How much of this 'wholeness' is revealed in the skull? Again with regard to the whole organism we may say, the underlying skeleton gives us the general structural plan, while in the boundary surface of the skin there are traced out for us the subtle delineations that mark out the particular man. Here, too, the skull differs from the rest of the skeleton. The bones of one man may be long and thin, those of another shorter and more compact, but the essential features are exactly the same; we know exactly what we are to look for, where each muscle finds its attachment, where the blood vessels enter, and so on. This is true of the skull also, but the skulls of human beings, unlike the other bones, show marked individual differences. Phrenologists speak of special bumps and they try to deduce from these bumps something of the character of the individual man. I do not think they are altogether right, but these individual differences are certainly there, and, whereas the skeleton as a whole can teach us secrets about man in general, the skull does contain secrets that apply to the individual.

Why do I think that phrenologists are not altogether right? They are not right if they try to judge a man from his bumps. Man is always something more, far more, than the eye can see. A man may have a so-called 'musical bump' but it does not follow therefore that he will become a famous musician, or that he will become a musician at all.

Another may have only the slightest indication of a 'musical bump' but patience and determination and hard work may carry him a good way further than his bump would lead us to suppose. And if this is true of the musical bump, it is equally true of any other bump or outer sign.

We all bring with us into life gifts in some directions and shortcomings in others but a man may fail in his gifts or he may conquer his shortcomings. We can never really assume anything from merely looking at the outside of a man. Nevertheless, the skull is unique in that it does certainly carry individual differences of form to a marked degree, and these differences must reflect something that belongs especially to the particular individual. This certainly adds to the feeling that when we are looking at a torso, a trunk, we see something that is more general, whereas in the head we see something that carries the general to particular completion.

The back of the head is rather like an egg, and it is as though out of this egg there were *born* the countenance. The back of the head is closed to us, it conceals something, whereas the countenance, by comparison, opens up to meet us. Can we ever imagine the face from looking at the back of the head? We cannot. The back of the head has untold possibilities, but the face is one single expression, one single possibility come to fulfillment. So we may say, the face we behold comes to meet us out of a past, a world that is hidden from us. Very much lies hidden in the countenance, too,—indeed much more than we can ever behold, but nevertheless, something of the hidden man is revealed to us, the hidden forces that have shaped the individual features flow out to us—the *character* of the man rests in no single feature but pervades them all. The countenance of a little child is hardly touched as yet by this hidden human being, but, as the years go by, his writing becomes clearer.

But now, what are the essential characteristics of the human skull?

How does it differ from any other skull? First we perceive the beautifully rounded dome of the upper head. When we look at the dome of St. Paul's, or at the dome of St. Peter's in Rome, what are we reminded of? Each is like a miniature heaven resting upon the solid masonry that rises up to meet it from the earth below. And so it is too with the human head. In all nature it is man alone that has this beautifully rounded dome as the crown of his upright, physical form.

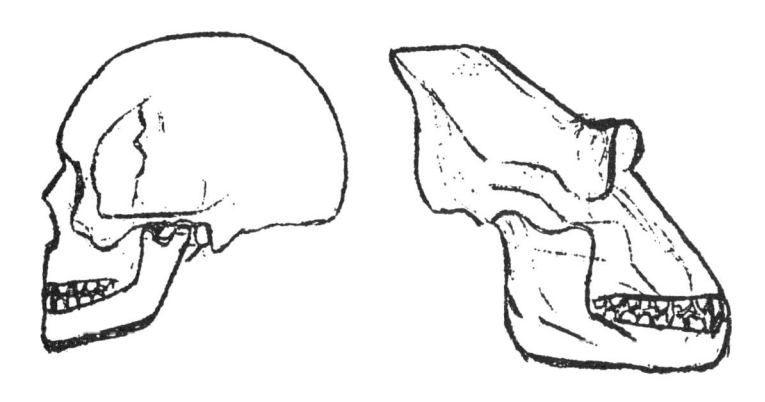

It is hardly an earthly form at all. Looking at this dome of the human head, above all the frontal part which is the special seat of human thinking, we may have the feeling: each man carries his own replica of heaven within him. And man alone possesses this, and possessing this, he is able to develop an inner life that carries him beyond mere physical existence—he is able to unfold a life of ideas and ideals within him.

In sharp contrast to this, behold the rectangular jaw below. An entirely different form! The same forces that fashioned the smooth upper dome could not have built this form as well. Other forces must come into play here. The clearly accentuated vertical line expresses something of the individual will. In it is expressed the force that raises man up from the horizontal position of the typical animal. The tiny child first raises its head, then its trunk, and finally lifts itself up on to its feet. It is the same force that lifts us up each morning—the force that makes us individually awake, so that we can take hold of our lives. In this vertical line of the jaw we may see how man gathers together that which is of heaven above and leads it down and concenters it in his own individual will. And, in the horizontal line, we go forward with this individual will to meet life, we advance forward into life to carry out the tasks that we have to do. Thus the upper part of the head is expressive of the free range of thought, the lower part mirrors the human will; these forms are by no means merely physical forms.

Between these two we have a most delicate structure, gently curved above and more articulated below, more head-like above, more limb-like below, expressing restfulness in the upper line and movement in the lower line, swelling forward into the cheekbone that swings upwards at the eye, tapering backwards and inwards towards the ear,—a wonderful bridge between the above and the below. This middle structure underlies that part of the face where the feeling life finds natural expression, the feeling that holds in balance the thinking and the willing.

In these three forms, the spherical form above that leads us back to the enclosed character of the back of the head, the rectangular form below that leads us down to the earth and forward into life, and the middle intermediary form that lends itself to both these, we have the essential character of the human skull.

We have but to glance from this to the ape to see the immeasurable loss. The frontal part of the skull, the dome in man, actually appears hollowed out, the rectangular jaw has lost its clean and concise angle and has become quite physical, and the delicate middle member has coarsened into a thick band of bony tissue from which all subtlety is excluded.

The human head, even in the rigid structure of the skull, is a true mirror of the higher soul forces that make man a kingdom apart and that distinguish him from all natural creation. Properly speaking, it is man alone that possesses a *head*.

(1964) — Francis Edmunds

(Reprinted from *The Michael Hall Journal*)

Bookbinding In The High School

A modern high school teaches bookbinding to Juniors and Seniors as a non-elective subject! Do these people want to revive the past? Who would want to bind old books with all the inexpensive editions overflowing the market? Aren't there more practical things that youngsters could do to prepare for college?

Questions like these will be asked by many people who hear about a school, a good school, a modern school, teaching, of all things, the lost art of bookbinding.

By rights one ought to invite these doubters to take the time to bind a book themselves. They would soon find out in how many ways this craft will help young people, not only on their road to college but on into life!

It was not easy, at first, to introduce bookbinding in the eleventh and twelfth grades in the Rudolf Steiner School. Many students had great difficulties in accepting this subject. However, very soon it was not only accepted but it happened time and again that some of the students came on their own after school—and even later, as college students during vacations,—in order to bind a book.

Laura, a Senior, came one day in the late afternoon to ask whether she might work on her bookbinding project. She needed badly to do that just *now*, as she had been preparing for tomorrow's mathematics test and was all tense and tired in her head. "To work with my fingers is the only way to become human again," she explained.

Bookbinding has this balancing quality, in common with many other crafts. Because of this quality, people who do strenuous thinking during the day often pursue hobbies in their leisure time. However, with most hobbies emphasis is put on attaining the desired end-result as quickly as possible, with the help of machines or the guidance of books that show how to get there "the easy way."

In a true craft—as in life itself—there is no "easy way," just as there is no short cut possible and no emphasis put on the end-result. In life, as in a craft, each step of the way is important.

In bookbinding everything is done by hand. As in geometry great precision is required. One needs to establish a close relationship with the materials involved. This relationship greatly resembles the one with other people. One has to be observant and tactful, do the right thing at the right moment, and rather than force one's crude will upon helpless materials, develop a feeling for when to do a thing and how to do it.

When paste is brushed on paper, the paper will curl up. A newcomer to the trade will think he has to counteract this curling as fast and effectively as he can. Gradually he will realize that the paper is acting like a naughty child and he will learn to wait until the "tantrum" is over and the paper has relaxed—which it does after a while. It can then be handled without difficulty.

In cleaning an old book, in taking it apart, in mending torn pages, the student will learn that he has to keep at it—but gently! Impatience, force, or negligence only bring about more tears and hence a greater repair job than originally was necessary.

Binding a book or making a box, a folder, or a photo album is done in many steps, which are very logical in their sequence. The students learn to see this logic and they also learn to plan the steps in their sequence.

Throughout the previous years they have done a great variety of crafts, developing considerable dexterity. Bookbinding represents, in a way, a culmination. In doing it one needs to think with one's whole being and particularly with one's fingertips.

It is necessary to balance intellectual abilities with sound feeling and controlled will. Daniel was a brilliant intellectual. In bookbinding he understood very well what he had to do. Yet he was incapable of even cutting two pieces of cardboard of equal size, with four right angles to each piece. John was a kind, friendly, very practical boy, academically a poor student, but his hands worked like magic; everything he did was very accomplished. Daniel would never have been able to bind a book without John's helping and watching over every step of his work. Both boys complemented each other. It did Daniel a lot of good not always to be the first, while John needed just that situation in which he could give his help out of the fullness of his heart. Here the best academic student depended on the poorest.

Maybe bookbinding does have something to do with life, after all.

(1971) —Margaret Frohlich

A High School Course in Child Study

An elective course called "Child Study" was first offered to the seniors of the Rudolf Steiner School, New York, in September 1970. A variety of factors contributed to the idea for such a course, but the major impetus was derived from a Kindergarten teacher's class report to the faculty. In this report she spoke of the interest, the concern, the willingness of the children's parents, but also—with the loss of the instinctive wisdom of past ages to guide us—of their confusion and sometimes utter helplessness in recognizing and responding to the real needs of their children. This, despite (or because of) the plethora of information available on child development.

The Child Study course, therefore, was initiated to focus directly on preparation for caring for young children and for the immense responsibilities entailed. Its aim is to learn to "read the child." Direct experience and careful observation are stressed. Through such "reading," awareness is heightened, and progressively deeper insights into the nature of the child emerge, so that the students, whether as future parents, aunts, teachers, social workers, or in any other capacity, can meet the child not as an animal, nor as a machine, nor as miniature adult, but as a unique developing human being.

While the course is purposely flexible, with content varying considerably from year to year according to the composition of the class, the schedule arrangements, etc., certain aspects of the work have come to be part of it every year. These include a broad view of child development through the three basic "seven-year" periods, and then special concentration on the all-important first phase of the child's life, when so much good, or so much harm, can be done. The question constantly before us is, "How can we create that environment in which the child can flourish?" In very specific terms, we deal with such fundamentals as feeding and clothing the child, his play and his toys, the role of sleep and preparing the child for sleep, the rhythms, the colors, music, activities in the child's surroundings, how to answer his questions, etc. We seek the answers to our own questions about the child in the child himself as we come to know "where he is" in his physical, emotional, social and mental development. We come to recognize the awesome responsibility of the adults to make every gesture, every tone, every attitude worthy of imitation—of that all-absorbing imitation which is characteristic of infancy and early childhood.

We also regularly include a study of fairy tales. Many fairy tales are read, several are discussed in detail, and each student prepares at least one fairy tale to tell to the Kindergarten children. A study of temperaments, of how to work with them and not against them, has received enthusiastic response (naturally the students first try to determine their own temperaments). In this connection our curative eurythmist and a teacher of form drawing have conducted lively lessons in which the students do the exercises and experience their impact. It has been particularly valuable, as part of the course, to scan the highlights of our curriculum through all the school years, showing how both method and subject matter arise out of "reading the child." Toward the end of the course we step over the boundary, outwardly marked by the change of teeth, into first grade, emphasizing when and how reading can be introduced. Some students bring their own first grade "notebooks" to be viewed through new eyes with fond recollections and delight.

The support and participation of many—class teachers, eurythmy teachers, handwork teachers, the school doctor, the school nurse—have provided vital elements of the course. Last year's class had the special joy of a surprise lesson with their former class teacher, who led them back to their early first grade days and their struggles with straight and curved lines. Above all, the Kindergarten teachers who welcome the students into their classes to observe, who guide them into participation in the Kindergarten activities, who meet with them to answer questions and to discuss the children or special topics, carry a major responsibility for the work. Frequently, they have arranged lessons in which the seniors are "Kindergarten children" for an afternoon of painting or working with beeswax or crayons, living into the experience as completely as possible. (The seniors have never washed the paint rags as well as the Kindergarten children!) In late spring the kindergarten teachers have sometimes arranged a display of the children's drawings and paintings from the very first weeks of school and on through winter and spring; and the students, now more adept at "reading," are able to discern secrets which would not have revealed themselves earlier to their eyes.

Each student usually carries out a long term observation of one child and writes as thorough and accurate a description of that child as he or she can. While each student spends at least one period and two or three full mornings in the course of the year working with the Kindergarten children, we wish there could be more time available for this essential experience. The "full mornings" are possible thanks to the support of their high school teachers who excuse the child study students from classes. Baby-sitting by some of the students provides additional experience.

Special projects by individual students or the whole class have included the making of dolls and toys and children's books, the making of puppets and the performing of puppet plays, and last year the class prepared a gift for all the younger children of the school—the fairy tale of "Little Red Cap" in eurythmy! During their visit to the Harlemville Farm*, the Child Study students have been graciously received into the work of the Kindergarten classes there, expe-

---

* Reference is to the work in Harlemville, N.Y. (some 120 miles north of New York City), which comprises a biodynamically-run farm, a hostel program, and the Hawthorne Valley School with Kindergartens and grades 1-12. Classes from the City, from Grade 3 upwards, spend a week or ten days there regularly each year. The Kindergarten classes referred to in this paragraph are precisely those of the Hawthorne Valley School.

riencing a different group of children in a different setting. One student spent a year after graduation as a Kindergarten helper at the Farm school. On several occasions, Child Study students have accompanied younger classes on their farm trips, serving as assistants to the class teacher.

Besides the primary purpose stated, the Child Study course (which would be more accurately titled "An Introduction to Child Study") helps seniors to put their past school experiences into new perspectives, forms a working link between the high school and the elementary school, and allows an opportunity for those seniors who have completed their language and math requirements to engage in a different kind of work. It is clearly a "culmination" fitting to the twelfth grade curriculum. History, art and science are all intimately connected in it. It is yet another approach to a knowledge of the human being.

(1978) —Nanette Grimm

The Value Of Art For The Adolescent

Before us on the screen is the figure of a Pharaoh. His body is uncomfortably still and rigid. He looks as if he were confined within an invisible strait jacket. His legs are stiff and parallel down to the toes, the feet flat on the ground. His weight rests on the back leg; we do not feel the urge to move arising within this man. His arms and hands are almost painfully harnessed to the body—no greater absence of freedom could be portrayed (even Michelangelo's Bound Slave is not so imprisoned). Lastly the head. The senses wide awake, full lips, large nose and nostrils, large eyes and ears, but there lies a secret: the eyes are not looking at you or me—they are gazing into space; their interest lies not in this world but beyond. They are not asleep, and not rapt in mystic reflection—the beyond is visible, a world of constant change, or filled with objects or beings that call forth respect and wonder. The head, whose importance is accentuated by the striking headdress, is slightly thrown back as though to emphasize the direction of the gaze into the beyond.

"Let not mine eyes stray from beholding thee, so that my deeds be but the expression of thy will."

We are spellbound by the tenseness and uprightness of the figure. And now we look at the same Pharaoh from behind. What a different picture! Most striking of all, it is a solid pillar from the very ground up to a point between the shoulder blades. There it changes to a thick, rope-like form composed of a series of rings; this in turn holds together, one might say controls, the whole headdress. Lines have their meaning—Egyptian sculpture makes this very clear—and the vertical lines of the pillar, resolved into the outspread, sun-like rays of the headdress, certainly give the impression of a personage who is held upright entirely by a force outside himself.

We have before us then someone quite different from ourselves, for—except for the medium held in a state of trance—we should certainly object if we felt we owed our upright stature to anything but ourselves. Is there anything in Egyptian history that would help us to understand this phenomenon?

The Egyptians, when asked by the Greeks who was their first king, replied, "King Menes." (3400 B.C.) "Who was King before that?" "Before that, the Gods ruled over Egypt."

Or take the Old Testament story of the Pharaoh and his dreams, which only Joseph could interpret. How insistent is the Pharaoh that the dream shall be interpreted! How else is he to know how to rule over Egypt?

So we have here a confirmation in art of something we know and can learn from history. The Egyptians stood differently in their relation to freedom than do we. If therefore all historical documents were destroyed, and only art were left, we should still have quite a lot to say about that time. Thus we confront art as a bringer of truth and knowledge.

And now, in striking contrast, we will look at a Greek sculpture, the statue of an Olympic runner. It is a maiden, yet we are not made specially aware of her feminine sex. What strikes us is the light poise, freed from material grossness, of the body on one foot,—the other ready to leap off; the hands slightly lifted, lifting the body as if on wings; a short garment with a series of delicate, fluidic, vertical folds, held together underneath the breast by a broad, quiet band; and the head with no particular expression, a familiar characteristic of Greek sculpture.

When the children see this, they are again and again seized and uplifted by the buoyancy of the figure, so light, so effortless, so rhythmical—the very essence of life and latent movement.

The Greeks knew how to form the body so that it could bear the stamp of the spirit. The lines run harmoniously, the forms are not infinitely removed from the 'ideal' form of the human body,—that ideal which in physical reality does not exist. And in beholding such harmony, we too begin to see more purely, to breathe more rhythmically, to will more 'lightly.' The shadow that so easily clouds the brow of the adolescent is dispelled: where life is so abundant, death has no entry. Art is beauty—the life-giver!

Lastly, an example from the realm of the painter. Most people know the head of Christ by Leonardo da Vinci from the Brera gallery in Milan. What does it express? We have before us a face with somewhat soft, feminine features. The eyelids seem to sink rather heavily; the nose is long, expressive of great feeling; the mouth so sensitive, there is almost a quiver on the lips. Lips that could pronounce words of such great contrast as those spoken to St. Peter, "Flesh and blood hath not revealed this unto thee but God," and "Get thee behind me, Satan,"—lips that could say, "Maiden, arise," and with those words command both life and death: such lips must needs be sensitive. But above all, the downward look, the seemingly heavy eyelids! What can divine goodness do other than lower the eyes before the weakness of humankind? These drooping eyelids are always waiting to be lifted that the gaze may fall direct on man, when man too shall be able to behold Him 'no longer through a glass darkly' but seeing 'face to face.'

With all this, there is no sentimentality in this picture, no weakness,—only patience, only the essence of goodness, only Christ as a child may imagine him.

Here art speaks the language of goodness.

And now let us turn to the curriculum of a Rudolf Steiner school and look up what it says about the adolescent. Here are Rudolf Steiner's words: "In the very age when the child has to learn to understand that nature is ordered according to abstract laws which must be comprehended through the intellect, when in physics he has to learn how cause and effect are connected in each particular case,—in this same age we should create a counterbalance through an understanding of art. We should introduce the child to an understanding of how the different arts have developed in the various epochs of human history."

And further we find the following paragraph: "Many of the difficulties and moral inhibitions at this age of the child's life which is so rich in riddles, wonders and surprises, and in which consciousness is striving to master the overwhelming life of feeling, can be surmounted by artistic and craft work, but also by lessons which are permeated by phantasy, enthusiasm and artistic feeling on the part of the teacher."

This last applies to the scientific subjects as well as to the humanities but nowhere so much as in the realm of art, where the human activity that has led to artistic creation is itself born of just these qualities of phantasy, enthusiasm and artistic feeling.

Artistic expression is something that lies deeply embedded in the human soul; it may take on many different forms of expression, but it is fundamentally a force to be considered and to be used. By allowing this force to remain dormant, by not giving it the right opportunities to come to expression, by not rightly releasing the pent-up enthusiasm, the hidden power of phantasy, the creative urge of artistic feeling, we stifle a vital part of the human being, and that which would otherwise add to life is obliged to find an outlet in forbidden ways. Destructiveness, nervous tendencies, pleasure-seeking, sexual difficulties, and many other errings of the adolescent can be found to originate in the lack or denial of this all-important factor in the totality of life.

It is a mistake to think that art is a luxury. Doctors emphasize the need for a correctly balanced diet for the body, and how the lack of this or that ingredient in our daily food leads to a corresponding weakness or even illness. Has a true psychology not yet discovered that the soul, too, needs its essential nourishment for its well-being?

Observe how children at the age of puberty develop physically more towards the earth, how the limbs grow longer, heavier, more ungainly, how the boys tend to slouch and the girls to stoop, how different this is from the freedom of movement and buoyancy of children of nine to eleven. And mentally, too, there is a change. Thoughts are developing by which understanding can be gained; but thoughts can also have a life of their own, they can be used for criticism, for peering into the shady recesses of human weaknesses, one's own as well as those of others or of the world in general.

And now recall the picture of the Olympic runner with its purity and rhythm. See how the forces of gravity, the down-pulling forces, are overcome—and so they can be overcome in the observer, too. Having taught art to adolescents over a period of sixteen years, I can say from experience that with each class in turn there has been a changed attitude towards life on the part of the children: the walk becomes different, the head is held higher. I can instance cases of children who have caused grave anxiety, who were sullen, stubborn, who would brook no guidance of any kind, and who, during the period on art, have become quiet, attentive, have gone out of their way to be generally helpful, and have devoted the utmost care and time to their notebooks. For such it would not be too much to say that the period on art was a turning point in their lives.

And let it not be thought for a moment that the study of art is essential only for the abnormal, the difficult or the intellectually weaker child. The effect for them may be more obvious, but I could equally well instance cases of highly intelligent children, who through their very force of intelligence were lifted away from their will-life and were in danger of remaining brilliant but ineffectual intellectuals. The interest in art, supported by the practical activities offered by the Waldorf curriculum at this time, awakened in them the desire—I would even say the faculty—for creative work and so proved to be for them the most healing thing that the school could give them.

It would be fatal to imagine that humanity divides into the artistic and the non-artistic. Life is a totality, and the life of the individual is a seeking to achieve this totality in himself,—and art, its perception, understanding and, if possible, its practice, is an integral member of this totality.

(1971)   —A. W. Mann

Caterpillar Capacities
Address to the Graduating Class of 1964 by its First Teacher.

Dear Seniors,

Just nine years ago, as you reminded me the other day, some of you were acting in a play on this very stage. You can still quote lines from it. Some of the boys were gnomes, the girls flowers, but Colin was the hero; he was Mr. Caterpillar! We had, at that time, been studying botany and the extraordinary parallel development of the plant and butterfly as they each make climactic changes from one form to another: from the seed-like egg, the sprout-like worm, the bud-like chrysalis to the flower-like butterfly. Toward the end of the play the gnomes came to look for their playfellow, Mr. Caterpillar, and found him, apparently dead, wrapped in a beautiful white shroud. Just at the height of the tragedy, as they were chanting, "The caterpillar's dead; we'll make him a bed, lay grass at his feet, a stone at his head," Colin with a mighty gesture burst straight through his white paper cocoon and appeared in his full glory as a most gorgeous butterfly!

What is it that happens silently and invisibly inside a cocoon? Scientists have delved into countless secrets of nature and put them to human use. Perhaps there are few secrets as mysterious and magical as this power of changing something ugly into beauty, something primitive into a wholly new and perfect form. What might we not be able to accomplish in the world if we could discover and make use of the laws which are at work in such a process?

Is it possible that man, like the caterpillar, already has such laws at his disposal? Yes, to some extent, for he can turn a desert into a garden, a stone into a statue, and with metal he can make music or a machine. The caterpillar, however, accomplishes a more difficult task. He exerts these forces upon himself. Do we also do this? Do we all our lives, perhaps, weave our experiences into the great cocoon of death—and then?

But I would like to ask whether man can accomplish similar transformations during his lifetime. Again, yes. We often say of some gifted student as he grows older, "His talents have blossomed." This is a very welcome but comparatively natural and easy development. The matured ability bears strong resemblance to its earlier, infant stage. Can man, however, go still further and change one form of soul into one of a quite different kind? An example of this more distinctive kind of transformation, taken from history, is the courage of the war-loving, young Saint Francis which changed into love of such vitality that it took him into the midst of the lepers in order to care for them. This is a change of one kind of strength into another.

A question which we all ask ourselves continuously, either consciously or unconsciously, takes us a step deeper still, into another level of ourselves. Is it possible to descend with this power into that region where our actual inabilities and weaknesses are lodged, where there is an unpleasantly soft and caterpillar-like formlessness, even evil? This question may remind you that it was the weak-voiced Demosthenes who became one of the greatest orators of Greece. I myself went to school with a girl who was older than the rest of us. In high school she still read very slowly and with difficulty. Today she is a greatly admired science teacher in one of the best private schools in New York. This autumn you read *Man and Master* by Tolstoy. In the end it was not the willing, unselfish servant, but the egotistical master, absorbed in his own gains as a merchant, who, by some strange alchemy, brought about in himself the desire and will to give his life for the man who had served him.

These are all examples, at various levels, of that kind of transformation which comes to such classic expression in the life of the caterpillar. What is the law at work here? Of what importance is it today? What is its source in ourselves? Here I would like to make a seeming digression in order to approach the answers to these questions from a new vantage point.

As you look today at the extraordinary brilliance of our modern civilization, you can realize that we owe a large share of its greatness to the incisive, clarifying powers of analytical thought, the ability to break down and divide things into smaller and smaller components. Never before have there been such advances in science, such speed of progress. The marvels of modern surgery, for which we can never be grateful enough, are based upon the analysis and dissection of the body, psychoanalysis upon the analysis of the soul. At the very same time we have to see that we are confronted by other divisions: the division between races, the cleft between East and West. Schizophrenia, the disease of the divided soul, increases: We have split the atom.

This modern world, in which analysis is such a prevalent and admirable trend, is not the world which you have formed. It is the result of the past and of other generations. What will be characteristic of the next epoch of civilization? We must not abandon analysis, but a strong counter-force is necessary if we are to bridge and heal those divisions which accompany it.

Now the caterpillar does not merely break down its own substance. He leads one form or expression of himself over into another, in continuing growth. This kind of change is called metamorphosis. Rudolf Steiner, the man whose methods of teaching we are trying to carry out here in our school, often spoke about the law of metamorphosis, and he made use of it. He applied it, for instance, to the architectural forms of a great building, the Goetheanum in Switzerland, which he designed; and he gave a particularly decisive illustration of it when he said that whenever anything evil can be turned into something good, then goodness of a very special kind comes about, goodness of a particular quality and strength. Perhaps we have all experienced this kind of goodness to a small degree when, after a quarrel with a friend, we have made an effort to reestablish the relationship and found that through the work and determination which we have exerted, the friendship has become realized and cemented as never before.

What is this artist in ourselves which descends into the unformed, incomplete, even weak and primitive parts of ourselves, but also into creative, mysterious, inexhaustible depths of our being and forms and re-forms us? Isn't this giant caterpillar our own individuality? It weaves what is undeveloped or deformed into a cocoon with the threads of clear thought, but then it broods over it, warms it and hatches it in the heart. Then certainly a very special kind of goodness comes about. This human caterpillar constantly makes over what is lower into something higher, the unconscious into the conscious, the purely racial into the individual, lifting man above nation, race and creed to a vantage point from which he appreciates rather than deplores the wealth of diversity which they create. Where individuality is at work, it is possible for men to work together and to work out their differences. Communion and community come about. When the individuality ceases to function, mankind becomes mob, and destruction and chaos result. It is interesting to note here that when people strive merely to be "different", a dreary kind of uniformity and mediocrity result, as in "personalized" Christmas greetings and so many dress design "originals", for instance; but when they exert themselves toward the same high goal, the good of their fellow beings, this effort proceeds, and can only proceed from the kernel of the individuality, which then stamps itself on every gesture and deed, as in the case of a Lincoln or an Emerson.

The thought that one phase of life, nature or a human being can change into another quite unlike what it was before, is a thought so human, so universal, that it is capable of bridging even the gap between East and West.

We had a striking example of this recently when we read together in class *The Bar of Shadow* by Laurens van der Post. You remember how, at the end of the book, the former inmate of a Japanese prison camp speaks to the man who had guarded and tortured him. After the war the Japanese guard—on the day before he is to be hanged—has sent for his onetime prisoner, who has already tried to intercede for him at his trial.

"I do not mind dying," says the Easterner, "Only please tell me what I have done wrong that other soldiers have not done, and I shall die happy."

And the Westerner tells him, "You can try to think only with all your heart that unfair and unjust as this thing which my people are doing seems to you, it is done only to try and stop the kind of things that happened between us in the war from ever happening again. You can say to yourself as I used to say to my despairing men in prison under you: 'There is a way of winning through losing, a way of victory in defeat which we are going to discover.' Perhaps that too must be your way to understanding and victory now."

And the condemned man answers, with the indrawn breath of recognition, "That is a very Japanese thought!" ... It actually was neither a Japanese thought nor a Western one, but a purely human thought.

So for a moment this recognition that the power of the individuality can change a thing even into its very opposite united the two men, the two races, the East and the West.

And now, at this joyful moment when you are about to burst the cocoon of your school days and try all kinds of flight on your wings in a world of a thousand new experiences, my wish for you is that you will take with you, and that you will never forget, your caterpillar capacities.

(1964) —Christy Barnes

Teaching Medieval Romances

In an era when all curriculum is being examined for its "relevance," Waldorf school teachers must often explain why they include *Parsifal* and other medieval literature in the third year of the high school curriculum. The following comments, based on my own experience in teaching these stories, may therefore be of some use to those who wish to consider this question.

It's quite true that young people like the stories uncommonly well and that not a few prefer them to current fiction. It may be the forthright and youthful style, or the appeal of the high and noble adventure, or perhaps the remoteness in time that pleases so greatly. And there may be deeper reasons, though these are not always appreciated at a first reading—not by the young or even the old.

The story of *Sir Gawain and the Green Knight*, of *Tristan and Isolt*, and of *Parsifal*,* are accounts of the trials to be endured and the achievement to be won by all who seek the Ideal. This quest is timeless, of course, and perhaps more actively sought by the youth of today than outer evidence would indicate. Rudolf Steiner, founder of the first Waldorf school, suggested in several of his lectures and books that *Parsifal* was, in fact, a story of the future development of mankind, and no doubt Richard Wagner was moved by the same conviction in composing his opera.**

Another reason for teaching *Parsifal* to sixteen- or seventeen-year-old students is that the study of a great quest seems to lead young people toward a quest of their own. It is no news that sixteen-year-olds want to understand themselves and to get some hint of their future. But it is news that today's sophisticated youth should find inspiration in a 12th Century romance, at least it was to me. I made this discovery when I first asked each student to write a story in the spirit of a medieval quest, as part of a three-week course. To my astonishment, students produced in a few days readable, interesting stories, some more than twenty pages in length, that seemed to flow from eager pens. These adventure tales about knights and ladies were written with varying degrees of earnestness, of imaginative power, and of insight—a few, of course, with tongue-in-cheek. Yet almost all the stories contained some clue of self-recognition, magically released by the medieval spirit and especially, I believe, by the study of *Parsifal*.

A few thoughts as to why students succeed in this venture: First, the well-established symbols, adventures, settings, and themes provide forms into which personal

---

* The text used is *Medieval Romances*, ed. Loomis (New York, The Modern Library, 1957). Unfortunately, this book is out of print. A replacement has not yet been found.

** For a fine study of this work, see Dr. Franz E. Winkler's article on *Parsifal* in Proceedings No. 21, Myrin Institute, 1968.

experiences can be readily translated. These forms satisfactorily camouflage the writer's own personality, yet provide the much desired clarification, the transcendence of life's perplexities, and even the humor with which to deal with them. In medieval stories 'shortcomings' such as jealousy, fear, pride, and laziness appear in brilliant dress. Yet they are set forth matter-of-factly, without censoriousness, and without psychological probing. Most young people find it is just the right tone, and one that is not difficult to imitate. The foolish questions and social blunders of Perceval in Chretien de Troyes' story, the flinching of Gawain before the Green Knight's blade, the evasions of Tristan, are viewed with sympathy by most high school students. Though they may be awakened to similar shortcomings of their own, the knowledge of them becomes less painful, and the hope of overcoming them becomes somewhat brighter.

While the medieval romances serve to turn one's glance inward, they can also open a way outward. Parsifal's bold undertaking of a mighty task speaks to all who would undertake their own life-tasks and responsibilities. The stories of the Grail knights, of their ideal of sacrifice and service, may actually be understood better by youth than by age. The Middle Ages have sometimes been pictured as the youthful period of Western man's development, before he achieved his full manhood in the Renaissance. It is certainly evident that medieval men, like the young, were all too heavily burdened by the demands of the flesh. Yet they understood the brotherhood of man and the Fatherhood of God with a particular purity and clarity never since equalled. In medieval romances these ideals shine as light through a stained glass window, now blue, now red or gold—depending on the position of the viewer. A fresh glimpse of them may make us feel as Perceval felt, when he first encountered knights in armor:

When he saw them clearly as they appeared out of the wood and observed the jingling coats of mail and the bright, gleaming helmets and the lances and the shields, such as he had never seen before, and when he descried the green and the vermilion catching the light of the sun, and the gold, blue and silver, he was so delighted that he exclaimed: "Ah, Lord God, have mercy! These are angels that I see."

Under such inspiration, a first step toward placing one's own talents at the service of others can be readily made. I like to think of the writing of a story as a symbolic act in this direction.

(1973)   —Jean Hamshaw

Mathematics In The Classroom: Mine Shaft And Skylight

I.

Towards the end of the first of eight lectures given in March 1921 to an audience consisting in large part of university students*, Rudolf Steiner describes three stages of human knowledge. The first is the ordinary or empirical observation and acceptance of the real world around us. The second is the penetration of the physical phenomena of the surrounding world with the help of mathematics. The third is the conscious, thought-clear experience of spirit at work in the world. In brief:

1. empirical study of nature
2. mathematical science and insight
3. science of spiritual reality

In the same context Rudolf Steiner recalls Plato's inscription over the entrance to his Academy in Athens: "Let no one

---

* Eight lectures published in German under the title of *"Mathematik, wissenschaftliches Experiment, Beobachtung und Erkenntnisergebnisse vom Gesichtspunkt der Anthroposophie,"* available in English translation as *Anthroposophy and Science*, Mercury Press, 1991.

ignorant of geometry pass through this door"—and reminds us that this injunction was not meant for prospective mathematicians or natural scientists. It was rather, as I would put it, a preliminary condition for a schooling towards the experience of the more than solid and eternal ideas of which our physical world, in Plato's parable of the cave, is but a shadowy image.

If this be so—if mathematics is indeed a gateway to supersensible experience—we are confronted by a disturbing paradox. For never has the river of mathematics flowed with such impetus and acclaim as it has from the seventeenth century to this day, and never, at the same time, have earthbound rationalism, materialism, reductionism acquired such dominion over the minds of men. Can we say that those who are especially trained in mathematics today are especially prepared to appreciate and understand knowledge of higher worlds? The opposite is more likely to be true. Why?

II.

This question, particularly for the teacher of mathematics, is of more than academic importance. My attempt to consider it in these few pages will be primarily from the point of view of teaching. But first, let us gain a little perspective by observing two other similar paradoxes. Is it not true that psychology, the science of the psyche, of the human soul, has often led in recent times to an explicit disavowal of the reality of the soul other than as a mere effluvium of physiological processes? And has not theology, the study of religion, of the divine, led in one of its extreme outposts to the declaration that "God is dead"? Since we must assume sincerity in the corresponding exponents of these views, we can only conclude that the two results are reflections of two actual experiences: the experience of soul as a mere "effluvium" (in oneself), and of God as being dead (in oneself). Surely one of the essentials of teaching is sincerity. To teach that which we teach without at least some nascent, own, inner perception of its truth or validity, would be hypocritical or worse. I would be a sorry professor of psychology who sensed no inkling of a soul reality in me, and yet taught that "the soul exists." In short, one prerequisite of teaching is to experience, at least incipiently, that which we would communicate or evoke in the student.*

III.

The efficacy of the teaching of mathematics, in our present context, depends then, in the first place, on *how we ourselves experience it*. It will depend, no less, on *how we teach it*. It is evident, to begin with, that mathematics in our times is generally experienced as a world of rational abstractions—abstractions, it is true, powerful enough to "split the atom" or take us to the moon—but experienced, nevertheless, as shadows in our mind. This is part of the more general experience of modern man, the experience of thought as void of substantiality and primitive reality, void of weight and being, certainly not to be compared with the intensity of an encounter with rocks and fire. Yet at the threshold of a new age groaning to be born lies Rudolf Steiner's affirmation that our thinking can and must be awakened and strengthened towards a conscious, daylight experience of its Atlas role in approaching the universe. And part of this experience is the rightly intuited idea. To awaken, in ourselves and in the student, a first experience of ideal reality—united with clarity of thought, and with several other elements of signal importance (see section VII)—is a very proper and pervasive task of the mathematics teacher.

---

* The understanding reader will realize that there are diverse categories of teaching matter, each requiring individual consideration. "The mean distance from the sun to the earth is 93,000,000 miles." Must I have a first, inward experience of this before teaching it? Not in the sense under discussion—yet the teacher should have a wakeful relationship to the nature of this statement.

IV.

I stand in front of a class of ninth-graders. With a piece of chalk, and a smooth, controlled movement of the hand, I draw "a straight line." (I joke with the class and ask them to imagine that I have drawn it "perfectly straight.") "But is this really a straight line?" I ask the class. "How long is a straight line?" It never ends, in either direction. It is infinitely long. What I have on the board, then, is at best a piece, a very small piece, of a line (a segment). But not even that. "How thick is a real line?" It takes a little time, perhaps, to face the fact that a real, a true, straight line, has no thickness at all. The chalk line on the board, however, has a palpable thickness—a measurable width and some height, too. It is really a mountain of chalk—an army of amoebas, say, marching down upon it, would find itself blocked by an insurmountable range or ridge of rocks. The real straight line is an ideal line, an idea! What more can we say about it? Remember how the "chalk line" got onto the board. Let me show it again. (I draw another chalk segment.) Yes—it is the idea of a straight line that works in me and guides me when, through an act of will, I move the muscle which moves the hand which moves the chalk which leaves a track, a trace, a sort of fossil on the board. The ideal straight line is itself invisible, colorless, weightless. It puts on a jacket of chalk, as it were, or of ink or of graphite, to make itself visible, to make itself manifest in the sense world. The ideal straight line is like a directing stream of force. A long, thin, strong cord, stretched taut between two students holding it, suggests (merely suggests) the quality of an invisible "line of force" inherent in the ideal straight line—the line which empowers human beings to build girders or a mile-long straight stretch of highway. All elements, all figures and forms in the world of geometry are, in reality, ideal elements, ideal forms.

Such considerations in class are auxiliary and passing, and must not be overdone. But whether an underlying sense of this is at least alive in the consciousness of the teacher, or no, will affect all teaching.

V.

Yet, if you reflect a moment on the "idea of a triangle," how else does it appear other than as a definition in words, as an elusive abstraction in the mind, which begins to have vividness and reality only when you draw an "actual" triangle with chalk or pencil, or cut it out in wood? Rudolf Steiner points in a different direction towards the experience of the concept of a triangle.* Let me suggest it in my own words. Imagine a screen or blackboard of cosmic size, reaching from rim to rim of the horizon. Let three "thin" lines of light appear on it, of limitless length, in three different, random directions, and forming thereby, in general, a triangle (with extended sides). Let the three "lines of light" begin to move, to sweep swiftly in all directions on the screen, to sweep in all directions with practically infinite speed. At this moment we begin to approach, at least to move in the direction of, the generative concept of a triangle. It is a dynamic, all-generating concept. For it contains, by arresting the moving lines at any one instant, any and all individual, representational or drawn triangles we can imagine, including the so-called degenerate cases of a triangle. The real idea of a triangle is anything but static and empty—it has, if anything, the quality of flame and fire.

Again, a point of light on the screen, opening into a small, thin ring of light and on into a growing circle that expands until it flows into an infinitely far horizon, then contracts again to become a point, pulsing thus from point through circle to infinite line and back to point in swift alternation,

---

* See, for instance, the course of four lectures given by Rudolf Steiner in Berlin, in January 1914, published in German under the title of *"Der menschliche und der kosmische Gedanke,"* lecture 1. Published in English, with the title *"Human and Cosmic Thought,"* by Rudolf Steiner Press, London, 1967.

likewise suggests a quality of the primal idea of a circle (though the Euclidian property of constant radius is missing in this description). It contains all particular circles—by arresting its movement at any moment, and paling it down into the sense world.

VI.

There are many occasions in class to implement, directly or indirectly, some awareness of what we have discussed so far. But that branch of mathematics known as Projective Geometry, which forms part of the curriculum in Waldorf Schools (often as a "main lesson block" in the eleventh grade), offers a special opportunity for it in various ways. Consider, as an illustration, the introduction of the so-called "elements at infinity." We begin with the "ordinary" straight line of Euclid, which extends indefinitely in two directions, and we find reason, by a series of historical and geometric considerations which we omit here,* to "add" a new point to it: the point at infinity on the line. This one point, in a clearly formulable sense, "completes" the line, makes it into a "closed path," and is such that we can say that two lines which are parallel in the Euclidian (ordinary) sense have a point at infinity in common, meet at that point. This, in the words of John W. Young, may strike one at first "as a very mystifying performance."** In effect, it is easy to divest the performance of mystifying aspects, but still leave open the question: what kind of reality, if any, can we attribute to "the point at infinity" on a line? The following demonstration helps us focus on the question. Near one end of a board which is four or five feet long and some eight inches wide,

---

* The seed of projective geometry can be found in the awakening and unfolding of the experience of perspective in life and in art, especially in the fifteenth century.

** See *"Projective Geometry,"* by John Wesley Young, a Carus Mathematical Monograph published by the Mathematical Association of America (1927 and 1929), page 12.

an upright (vertical) glass plate is fitted with two thin, opaque "lines" marked on it crossing one another at point P (see Fig. 1).

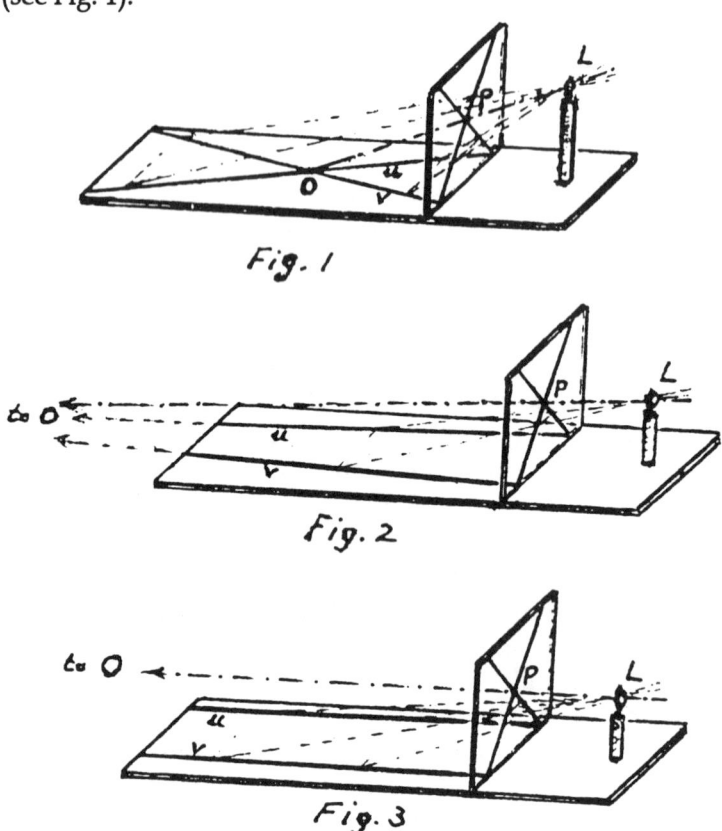

Fig. 1

Fig. 2

Fig. 3

A point-source of light L* is placed behind the plate at a proper height, so as to cast the shadow of the cross-lines on the board in front of the plate. The shadow shows two dark lines, u and v, crossing or meeting at point O (Fig. 1). Let us gradually lower the light source L. We *see* the shadow lines u and v separate outwards, as it were, and the cross-point O

---

* The point-source of light is represented only symbolically in the drawings by the flame of a candle.

moving away (to the left) from the plate on the board. As we lower L still more, the cross-point no longer appears on the board; it recedes faster and faster, and we can only *visualize* or *image* it, farther and farther out, as the shadow-lines diverge more and more (Fig. 2). There comes a moment (when the height of L above the board equals the height of P above the board) when the shadow-lines appear clearly parallel (Fig. 3). What has become of the shadow point O of P at this moment? Can the shadow of two cross-lines be two non-crossing lines? We can, by an effort of imaginative thought, conceive the shadow-point to be still there—but infinitely far away. It is now the point at infinity common to the two lines u and v; and we can no longer see it with our senses, we can no longer visualize it even, we can only *think it*. (It is intriguing to ask: what if the light source L is lowered still more?) Three stages:

1. Perceiving
2. Visualizing or imaging
3. Pure thought

At this point we can ask again: what is the reality of the point at infinity, now apprehended in "pure thought"? The answer cannot be given dogmatically. But we can, as teachers, point to the mathematical fruitfulness of this concept (which will appear in the further development of the subject), and suggest—again undogmatically—two paths that open up to us in answer to this question, one of which leads to the possibility of higher stages of reality.

VII.

Let us note explicitly, to avoid misunderstanding: our teaching of mathematics in the classroom must do justice to many aspects of the subject. It will include, in a Waldorf school, the content and substance of the standard math courses, presented at various points perhaps in a new light or with new emphases, and supplemented by other units of significant mathematical and math-related work. It will strive to be versatile and comprehensive: seeking to cultivate the clear, controlled power of logical reasoning; exhibiting the presence of mathematics everywhere in the world of nature and man (natural laws, science); drawing from history a sense of mathematical and human development; including awareness of the beauty and ordering power of mathematics (cf. a chambered nautilus, a rose window, a snowflake). It must, of course, develop skills and techniques in the student that are needed in everyday life today and tomorrow, and give a proper appreciation of the practical power of the subject in our time (technology, statistics, computers). In much of this we shall see mathematics as a shaft reaching deep into the mines of our earth existence, to bring out the many treasures just described. At the same time, we should recognize in it also a skylight opening up to a light that shines from above in the sense of the first six sections of this article.

We must be careful. All that we have said and implied in those first six sections is not content to be imparted to the mathematics student. It is a potential pointing to ideal reality which resides in mathematics and whose experience cannot be commandeered into existence. But it can be overlooked and neglected and even denied. How it may be made real—without dogma, without insincerity—must depend on the experience and the pedagogical tact of the individual teacher.

(1982) —Amos Franceschelli

Reprinted from the *Journal for Anthroposophy*, Spring 1982, with kind permission of the editor.

Grace At Meals

A talk given to the High School students at the Waldorf School of Garden City

The Student Council has asked me to set its new project in context with a few words concerning the meaning of grace at mealtimes. As you know, the Council hopes to introduce the custom of a silent grace into the high school's luncheon period. Because this will not be easy to do in a cafeteria, and will require forbearance, persistence, and ingenuity, the Council is especially anxious to have the importance of the effort clear in our minds.

I should like to support the idea of offering thanks before eating by two considerations, one of manners, the other of health.

We know that in ancient times blessing was asked not only upon the meal but also upon the harvest that made the meal possible—and, indeed, upon the very act of breaking the earth and planting seed that makes the harvest possible. Thanks were given, blessing was asked, when a fishing boat or fleet set out for the catch. This latter custom continues to this day. And in many homes, though not the majority perhaps, some form of grace is still being asked upon the meal. The breaking of bread together is still regarded by some as a sacrament.

Now despite the fact that our present culture does not have much feeling for the sacred, for such a thing as grace at meals, when we sit down at the table we are still expected to be gracious. It is not good form to sit down first, to reach out farthest and fastest, to chew loudest. We are not to grab, not to rend and tear, not to display too much appetite. The *human* style is not to hog and not to wolf.

Can graciousness be preserved without grace? Ultimately, I think not. A code of manners becomes empty and insincere, and it will eventually crumble, unless it is supported from within by real feelings. Table manners should be the way one naturally acts when he bears himself with the simple dignity of a spiritual being, when he warms to the spiritual presence of his companions, and when the food to be eaten by all is regarded as a wonder and a blessing. Such alive awareness sets the tone, and it shapes the smallest details of gracious behavior.

I do not believe graciousness can endure except upon the foundation of gratitude for grace received. One may be grateful at mealtime to the men who have grown the food, to the women who have prepared it, to the plants and animals themselves whose body becomes our sustenance. One may be grateful to the sun that holds and shines upon all, to the air and water that make growth possible, and even to the very rocks that patiently support our planetary existence. One can sense wisdom and love in and through all of these provisions.

It is not easy in our day to take the time needed to remember our benefactors and let thanksgiving grow in our hearts. But it is worthwhile. By such an act we master life. In this mastery lies the meaning of our whole existence. To give thanks before eating is one of many acts of initiative by which we establish human values, overcoming instinct by purpose, routine by fresh awareness, and pressure by peace.

If good manners affect the health of society, they also affect our own health. As you have already heard from a fellow student, we can no more take for granted that the ingestion of food will lead to the right building-up of our bodies than we can trust that the crude rush of external events will of itself shape into a noble society. Food must be assimilated, and it must also be blessed, if the lower forms of vegetable and animal substance are to become human flesh.

In the work of digestion the teeth do their part, and the tongue, and the juices. These reduce the original form of foods to zero and slowly build them up again in the image of man. When the breakdown is complete, and nutritive substance enters the blood, the upbuilding begins. The liver contributes to this, and the air we draw into our lungs. But these unconscious processes do not complete the rarefaction, permeation, and transformation of foreign substance into the noble, delicate human body. So subtle a thing as our mental attitude, the quality of our thoughts and feelings, also plays a decisive part.

To digest food properly we must be "all there." Not only must the appropriate organs be functioning; we ourselves, in the warmth of our ideal striving, must be present. This warmth will, or will not, penetrate every cell and tissue. If it does, our health will be more likely to rise above certain of the illnesses that characterize our unmastered, unhumanized time.

We are all aware that great successes have been achieved in suppressing and eliminating infectious diseases; but we know, too, that with every year that passes the so-called degenerative diseases have advanced. They set in at ever younger ages; they claim ever more victims. I am referring to heart disease, arthritis, cancer, and some forms of mental illness, for example, depression. We could include obesity, the accumulation of excess fat, which has become prevalent in America. What do all these illnesses have in common?

I am not a doctor, of course, and it is dangerous even for doctors to generalize. Each degenerative illness has its own specific cause and character: e.g. arthritis results when calcium is deposited in the joints; hardening of the arteries, when cholesterol is deposited along the lining of blood vessels; senility, when the brain itself calcifies. Cancer occurs when bodily tissue grows beyond its natural limits—the limits that indicate the controlling, formative presence of the individual who lives in this body.

I will risk saying that, regardless of the differences between these diseases, they have in common an incomplete or imperfect metabolism of some kind. When blood does not flow freely, joints do not move smoothly, muscles are layered in fat, and certain tissues overgrow, we feel a lack of complete combustion. We are reminded of a fire that does not burn brightly but smokily.

I hasten to retreat from medical pronouncements, yet I cling to the idea that the experience of appreciation, gratitude, and thankfulness while partaking of food can help supply that last measure of warmth and control that will first destroy and then rebuild this food into a noble form. This warmth will enable us to penetrate the processes of our own body through and through. It will establish our presence in every cell, tissue, and organ.

There are many ways to use the moment of silent grace. At the very least, we can practice self-recovery by assuming a composed, alert posture. We can formulate thankful good wishes and send them where the heart directs. We can pray for guidance to use for good purposes the strength we gain through the sacrifice of many beings.

(1970) —John F. Gardner

Table Prayer

The plant roots quicken in the night of the earth,
The leaves unfold through the might of the air,
The fruit grows ripe through the power of the sun.

So quickens the soul in the shrine of the heart,
And man's spirit unfolds in the light of the world,
So ripens man's strength in the glory of God.

Rudolf Steiner

(Translation by Michael Jones in *Prayers and Graces*, Floris Books, Edinburgh.)

IV
THE WHOLE SCHOOL

.... When we bring to the child, just at the right moment, matter appropriate to his faculties, to his disposition, then what has been thus introduced will become a re-creating source of refreshment for the child throughout the whole course of his life.

If the parents of our children perceive that we have the will to work in such a way that we place into the decades lying before us people capable of dealing with the ever-increasing difficulties of life—but still having questions to ask of life—then the parents will stand in the right relationship to the school. For it is upon the parents' understanding that we must build. We cannot work, as do other schools, protected by the state or by any other authority. We can only work supported by a community of parents who have this understanding ...

We love our children; our teaching is inspired by knowledge of man and love of children. And another love is being built up around us, the love of the parents for the true essence of the school. Only within such a community can we work towards a future of mankind able to prosper and withstand.

Rudolf Steiner
(From an address to parents of the
first Waldorf School, January, 1921)

Drawing: From First Grade To High School

The following study is an attempt to shed light on the whole complex of drawing as practiced in a Waldorf school. There is no intention to give drawing a preferred position, nor is there any desire to establish a fixed curriculum. It is merely an outline of what is available on the subject.

One of the first and most important impressions of the little First Grader on beginning school is his introduction to the straight and the curved line, and to color. Two mighty streams, one can say, like two mighty helpers, are going to accompany the child through elementary school. One of them bestows on him the flowing world of color; the other leads him to the severe, pure form of the line. Here only the line as an independent means of expression is to be studied.

The straight and the curved line, which Rudolf Steiner proposed as an approach to the first lesson, are the most simple elements of the art of drawing. But one should not judge them as merely 'simple' because the grown-up can easily handle and copy them. We should rather ask: what do these two signs seem to express? Anyone who takes up drawing will make the interesting discovery that the two lines represent the archetypal motifs of the art. We stand at the fountain-spring. With these two lines, combined and varied, we can represent the whole universe of objects, and any freely imaginative composition as well. Each of the archetypal motifs is a whole, and

Fig. 1

each embodies polarity. As the strongest opposites of expression, their union can demonstrate complete harmony.

When the child has practiced for a time and concerned himself with these two motifs, he can be led by his teacher toward simple geometric forms. The straight line can be combined with other straight lines to form a triangle, a square, a pentagon; the curved line can become a circle, an ellipse, lemniscate, a spiral. (Fig. 2)

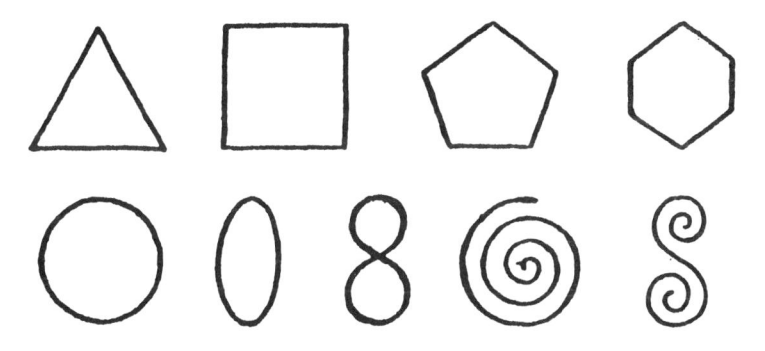

Fig. 2

Out of these fundamental forms, more complicated forms can develop, for example through overcrossing. (Fig. 3)

Fig. 3

Exercises in which one half has to be completed by the child can also be started. They will assume more and more importance later on. Like all exercises in form, they will not only make small hands more skillful and the eyes more sure, but they actually quicken and strengthen the thinking forces, and help the child in learning to write and read. The fact is, they help the soul of the child to catch hold of its body in the right way. These are forms of which one half is drawn by the teacher; the missing halves have to be completed by the child. (Fig. 4)

Rudolf Steiner said in the Ilkley Course:* "We can start even with the smallest children in this way. We draw such a half-figure on the blackboard, put down the center a helpful middle line, and then begin to draw for the child a little of the symmetrical side. We should try to make the child see that the drawing is not finished but must still be completed. By every possible means the child should be persuaded to finish the drawing all by himself. In this way you awaken an inner active urge to complete something as yet unfinished, obtaining thus a command of the child's own inborn sense for reality. For this the teacher needs a good deal of ingenuity, but this is something a teacher should have in any case! The first requirement of any teacher is a lively, inventive thinking capacity."

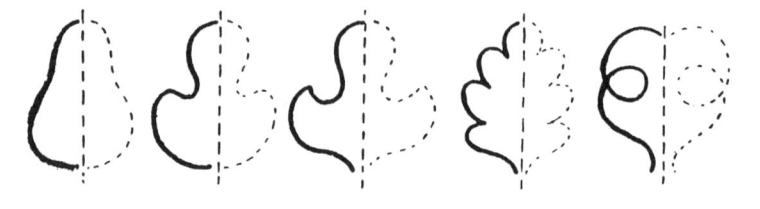

Fig. 4

Similar to the symmetry exercises are the forms which arise as mirror-images (see the Torquay Course).**

Besides the symmetry and mirror exercises, one can start to practice—perhaps from the Third Grade on—the somewhat more difficult metamorphosis-forms, which are mentioned in the same lecture. Here too our task is to enlarge and widen the stimulating suggestions given. Designs should be

---

* Lectures given at Ilkley, Yorkshire, in August, 1923: published as a book, *A Modern Art of Education*, Rudolf Steiner Press, London 1981. See Lecture 9.

** Rudolf Steiner, *Kingdom of Childhood* given at Torquay, Cornwall, in August, 1924. See Lecture 4. A few examples of this are given. (Fig. 5)

transformed in such a way that out of a harmonious parallel movement, a harmonious asymmetrical counter-movement is created (Fig. 6a and 6b).

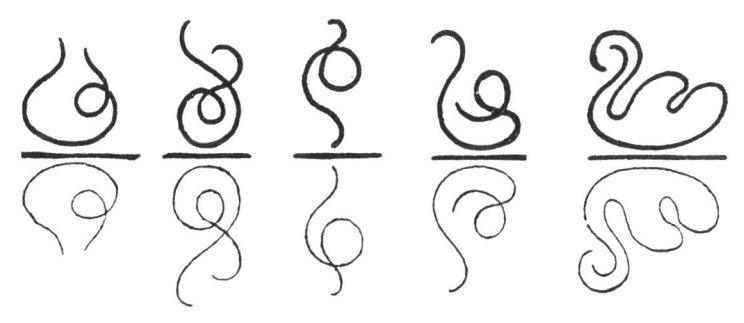

Fig. 5

Fig. 6a   6b

In the above-mentioned Ilkley lecture, Dr. Steiner continues: "When the teacher progresses to other exercises, he may draw some such figure as this (Fig. 6a) on the blackboard, and then try to awaken in the child an inner spatial idea of it." Here the three arcs constitute an entirely harmonious, symmetrical figure, which is filled out evenly in the center by an equally harmonious, symmetrical threefold loop. Now the teacher should transform the three partial circles, so that each one changes into a three-lobed leaf. In this way a free, very flowing, organic form arises. There is no more symmetry in the strictest sense of the word; we have progressed to a more plantlike, living form. The teacher will have to explain to the child that when the outer form is varied, the inner one must also be changed accordingly. What should become of the inner loops of Fig. 6a? In the whole figure we have a harmonious parallel movement of the outer and inner forms. We can say an outer harmony is reigning. In the second figure it should be metamorphosed to an inner harmony. In order to attain it, countermovements have to arise; i.e. where there is a convex movement, the inside answers with a concave movement. Stress arises between inside and outside. There follows a concave movement outside and a convex movement inside. Harmony ensues when they meet and continue together. Instead of the harmonious parallel movement of Fig. 6a, we have now from without and within a living harmony of stress and balance.

Figures 7a and 7b show still more strongly the hidden metamorphosis taking place. The teacher draws 3 fishlike shapes, which strive toward a center point, and adds 3 outer shell-like shapes. And now we open out the shell forms so that both ends seem to run into indefinite space. The child should be brought to form a lively idea of how, through opening the 3 outer shapes, a strong movement towards the periphery has come about, so that he himself has to run after the lines into infinity. Because of this escaping, there must be a definite counterbalance on the inside, and here the 3 inner forms bring themselves together into an entirely new shape. In 7b a new form has come into being which seems, if one glances at it only superficially, to have little to do with Fig. 7a.

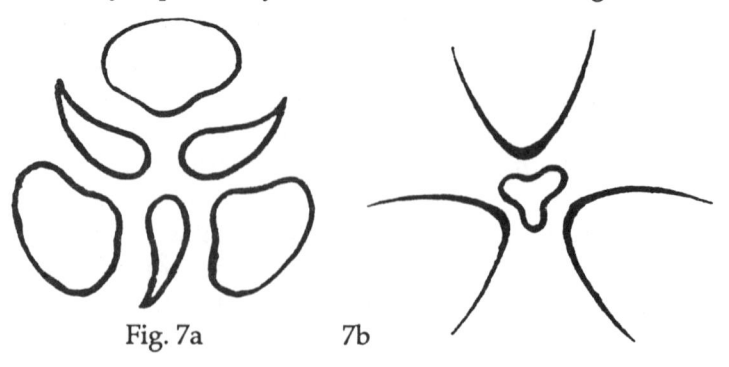

Fig. 7a   7b

We enter here into the working of a metamorphosis, which—if we follow it closely—lets us guess perceptively at the secret of a hidden movement, and even too brings hidden forces and activities into movement in the human being. Inward activity and creativity arise, processes are stimulated which have a strengthening effect on the health of the organism. What the child experiences in his efforts to bring about such forms, he takes with him into sleep. During our sleep we digest or clarify the things we were busy with during the day. Thereby the forms do not come to rest, but continue to vibrate and become more perfect. Out of his sleep then, the child brings new capacities for learning and experiencing. Thus even into the physical body, this method of learning to draw has a quickening and health-giving effect.

In the same category of form-metamorphosis belongs the following motif from the Torquay course of lectures (Fig. 8a, 8b). Here is shown how a change from the outer curved lines, in 8a, to the outer angular lines, in 8b, demands also a change in the inner lines which the child should be asked to find for himself.

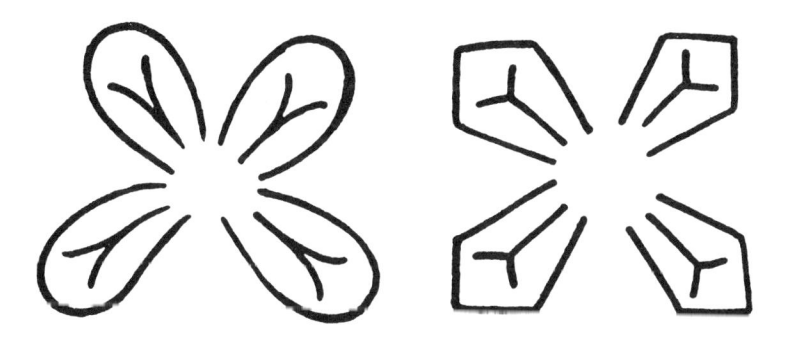

Fig. 8a   8b

Another very rich field for free forms is that of the so-called ribbon motifs, of which Rudolf Steiner gave a few examples for crafts-work. Those shown in Fig. 9 are freely invented and express significantly the difference of the straight and the curved line.

Fig. 9

The much discussed "book corners" should also be practiced as free forms, especially when they are going to be used by the children on their notebooks. One starts primarily from the artistic *function*, which should be expressed by a rounding, protecting motion at the upper left, and with more of an invitation towards opening in the right hand corner below, where one turns the page. The printing itself should form an artistic whole with the design. The use of straight lines will lead to severe angles, while the curved line will show a more dynamic, flowing movement. A certain artistic-architectural strength should be observed, even with the more rounded designs, and it is clear that the corner-form should have an artistic relation, not merely a symbolical one, to the contents of the book. That this is not easy will be noticed immediately by anyone attacking the problem. (Fig. 10)

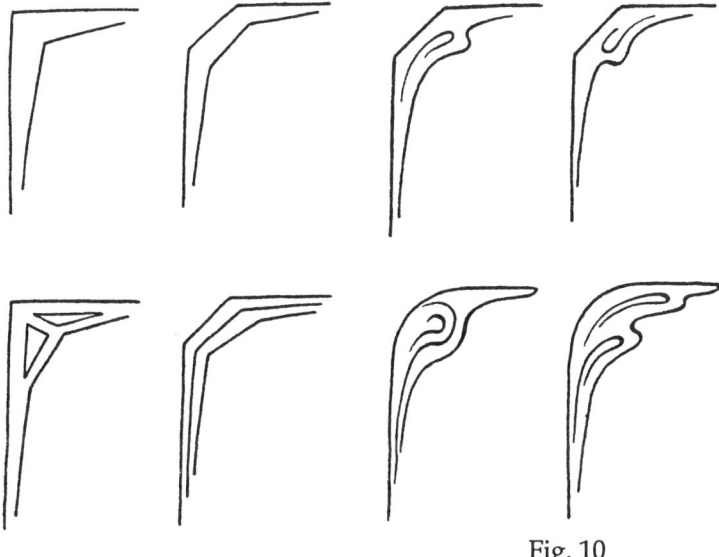

Fig. 10

This kind of free form drawing can be used in various ways from Grades 1 to 8 as it is needed. From what has been said so far, it is evident that in the free form, the line has a significance entirely its own, as an independent means of expression: it should not be confused with a line of contour, or outline. Here the line remains something alive and artistic in itself, even though, in contrast to the expanding character of color, the line is concentrated and one might say, drawn into itself. From this we can see the pedagogical situations where drawing should be useful: it brings about in the child also a concentration, a drawing into himself, which coming from an artistic medium will strengthen the child's moral attitude.

If we have experienced in this way the realm of free form as an absolute unity, the question arises: How can we unite this realm with the drawing of objects, and especially with "copying Nature"? The drawing of chairs, tables and similar objects, with light and shadow, can be taken up in the Sixth Grade, even without any knowledge of perspective, if the above-mentioned sense of form has been sufficiently developed beforehand. The child then will not be overwhelmed by the object, but will be able to study the different angles that arise.

Perspective itself should take its start from the geometry lesson, as Dr. von Baravalle has expressed it in the preface of his book, *Perspective*. Let us look perhaps at the question of the importance of perspective. After two centuries of preparation, it was out of the painting of the 15th century that perspective appeared and had its laws formulated. In painting we speak of the birth of naturalism, which climbed to its highest triumph in the 19th century. It is an ever stronger grasp on outer reality. What, however, is hidden behind it? What has been found through perspective, and what becomes visible through it? It is the third dimension of space, that of depth; in the human being, it is the dimension of the will, experienced for one thing in walking forwards and backwards. Graphically spoken, its real nature can not be represented—therefore it can seem like a genial joke of the intellect when the two-dimensional surface is used to bring into appearance the third dimension. When the illusion is there, the surface is, so to speak, invalidated, annihilated. Something decisive has happened, for in ancient times, was not the surface the medium to represent imaginations? Perspective destroys the surface, and with it the imaginations as well, and drawing lands finally at the imitation of the outer world. One can value this negatively; as in all the spheres conquered by the intellect, old values must be destroyed. But through this a definite step forward towards the freedom of the human being is made.

We see children who have reached the age of physical maturity in a similar situation. The intellectual forces have fully awakened and with these the urge is increasingly and ever more strongly to lay hold of the world around them; at the same time they wish to throw off all the restraints and compulsions of childhood. It is of great benefit to them then, and a comfort, to use drawing as a medium of expression. With it children can approach the world, which is so full of riddles, from a new angle. The feeling for form and a sensitivity for the expression-values of the line have been nurtured and developed. Now they lack only a knowledge of perspective in order to represent the outer world of objects in the way that will satisfy intellectual needs. The inherent danger of this step should not be underestimated. The quantitative perspective can easily push children entirely into the physical world, and they will then be given up exclusively to space and matter. But there is one means of protection, and that is color. For years they have experienced qualitative perspective and the dynamics of color-depth. This should help protect them from being sucked out altogether into the physical world.

There is another protection for children from being overwhelmed by the multitudes of new form possibilities: it is the wealth of expression gained through frequent exercises in free form drawing. In the shape of a vase, for example, the top and bottom will be recognized as flat ellipses, while the outside curves will remind the children of the often practiced symmetry exercises. (Fig. 11)

Thus the drawing of objects will not become painfully difficult, but will prove a joyous recognition of well-known form elements. The danger that the innocent

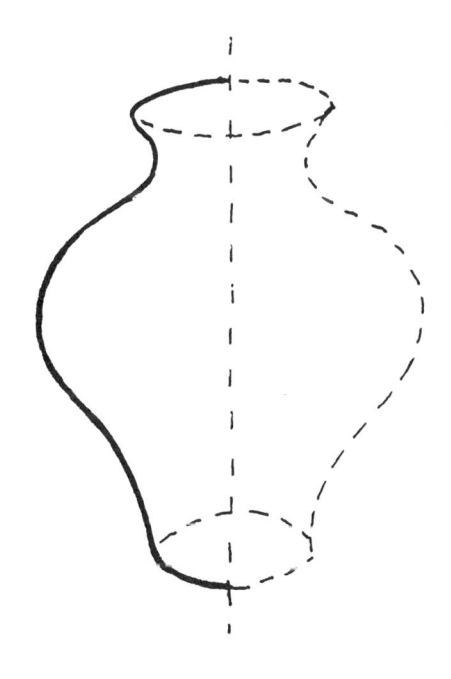

Fig. 11

forces of the child's soul might be violated by the sensational magnitude of the physical world has been reduced to a minimum.

Drawing from nature in the Eighth Grade is by no means, however, the goal of the drawing lessons, but merely a more or less intensive transition study. In Grades 9 and 10 it will be replaced by something entirely new: charcoal or black and white drawing. Now the aim is no longer to realize an object by means of line, perspective, and shadow—instead, the light and dark surface itself will lead to artistic expression without an external model. In this technique, surfaces are formed by a differentiated use of diagonal hatching, and it has two notable characteristics. First of all, while dealing with the three-dimensional object, it remains in the artistic two-dimensional realm, and therefore does not sink into naturalism. Secondly, it remains—even in its depths of darkness—transparent to light. (Fig. 12)

Fig. 12

These two things in black and white drawing are most important, the finely artistic quality and the light which is brought about by means of a black crayon. With the help of this technique children can best bring to objective expression the contrasting light-dark problems of the soul, problems inherent at this age. With its help the strong emotional contrasts and conflicts can be reconciled and overcome.

Summary

A. The starting point for all drawing:
   the straight and the curved line .... *1st Grade*

B. Free forms as a basis for drawing
   1. Simple geometric forms............................*1st to 6th Grade*
   2. Supplementary exercises
      (symmetry, etc.)..*1st to 6th Grade*
   3. Metamorphosis of forms ....*1st to 6th Grade*
   4. Ribbon motifs...*1st to 8th Grade*
   5. Book corners... *4th to 8th Grade*

C. Perspective and object drawing
   1. Object drawing without models, simple
      projections and construction of shadows
      (see curriculum of 6th Grade)...........................*6th Grade*
   2. Perspective drawing: geometry to
      simple pictures .... *7th and 8th Grade*
   3. Drawing from nature (artistically
      used perspective)..*8th Grade*
   4. Action and object drawing in other
      classes (botany, zoology, physiology,
      geography, history, art history) .... *3rd to 12th Grades*

D. Illustrations with colored pencils
   (close to painting)*.................................. *1st to 5th Grades*
E. Charcoal drawing ....*9th and 10th Grades*

(1959)   —Carl Froebe
(Translated by Rudolf Copple)

---

* Not described in this article.

History Teaching—A Dramatic Art

It is to the great dramatists—Molière, Schiller, Shakespeare—that the teacher of history turns for inspiration in preparing his lessons. They can help him to distinguish the essential pattern from the mass of unrelated facts. Like them, he has to become a master of economy if in his presentation the underlying dramatic movement of history is not to be lost sight of, beneath the shifting surface of events.

Modern historical research has unearthed quantities of facts concerning the life and thought of men in the past but, as happens in some museums, the mind of the student is stifled by sheer accumulation. Only when some thinker possessed of the lightning flash of genuine historical insight and dramatic imagination resolves the mass of facts into meaningful connection, can the ordinary student understand what it is all about. And until he can do this there is no hope of ever arousing his enthusiasm for history. Without this enthusiasm there can be no deeper interest in the destiny of mankind.

The growing materialism of the past centuries has spread its pall over our understanding of history. We have been taught to recognize only the outer shell of human development. We know all about the evolution of tools from the stone age to the modern machine. Transportation, communication, housing, dress, all the techniques of life, have been traced from their most primitive forms. The history of society is evaluated as class struggle, as mere struggle for power: survival of the fittest. All human impulses have come to be derived from the economic and the physical instincts. But what about the spiritual history of man?

In exact proportion to the progress of external research the perception for the spiritual evolution of man has faded. How often it is said that "human nature has never changed". It is also said that, fundamentally, men are the same today as they were under the Pharaohs, only now life is more complicated. A terrible levelling of historical perspective has taken place and we no longer are aware of the differences between one epoch and another. We fail to recognize the gulf which separates the Greek from the Egyptian and the latter from the men of earlier cultures. The idea that each culture had its own task in the development of man, that something entirely new entered into each era and that there is a goal for mankind underlying historical evolution has become unfamiliar to us today. History has become, in the words of Nietzsche, "an endless repetition of the same". If in our schools we want to prepare children for life, if we want to awaken in them a creative idealism which will not flinch at reality, we must find a new understanding and presentation of history.

When a class teacher in a Rudolf Steiner school is preparing his first period of actual history, to be given during a concentrated sequence of five or six weeks sometime during the fifth grade year, he will have to cover much the same ground as does his high school colleague who may be presenting the same material. But the elementary school teacher will use the material in a different way. He must remain within the sphere of the imagination in his way of presentation. He will tell the stories of the past; he will make frequent use of biography and always he will try to recreate the characteristic mood of the historical period with which he is dealing. His lessons, then, will stir the feelings and arouse the slumbering will-power of his pupils, with the result that in their adult years this early experience of history will have been transformed into moral capacities for life.

If, for example, a teacher wants to give children of ten and eleven a feeling for the character of Egyptian and Greek culture, he will treat it as a dramatic problem and will seek opportunities to present certain essential contrasts between the earlier and the later civilizations. The facts of ancient history can be gathered in every good library; the question is, how they can be made to come alive in the mind of the teacher. After the textbook has yielded the necessary information, it will be put aside, for nothing interferes more unhappily between teacher and pupils than the foreign authority of the printed page. The teacher must first master the material and then present it to the children quite spontaneously. Unless he is genuinely enthusiastic about his subject he need never expect to awaken the enthusiasm of his students. What follows here will have the character of marginal notes made during the course of preparation.

In meeting a character in a drama for the first time, we turn our interest to his outward appearance: stature, coloring, features. In history we can do this also. Let us look first at the two lands which were to be the homes for the Greek and Egyptian cultures. The geographical facts are familiar to all of us. But how can we get the most out of them?

Will we first hang up a printed page and say: This is Egypt . . . This is Greece? On the contrary, let us sketch their portraits! An hour or two spent in drawing the map of Egypt and of Greece, free-hand and in color, will teach us more than any amount of poring over someone else's work. Like the children, we will be delighted with the forms of the land masses and our imagination will guide our hand as we fill in the deserts with ochre and sandy yellows, the meadowlands with green, the rugged mountain spines with brown. The Abyssinian mountains are even capped with snow near the equator! There is hardly a rounded curve in the whole indented coast of Greece! All the lines are sharp and jagged. Our struggling fingers tell us that these promontories are not sand nor soft stone nor earth, but hard, original rock against which the waves have beaten for centuries.

If we are not fortunate enough to have been to Greece and Egypt ourselves, we will try to see them through the eyes of other travellers. Egypt is almost two-dimensional. It has no breadth. The Nile is all. Should it fail to rise, the desert would complete its victory. Above the cataracts is a land of mystery. There all life begins. There the Nile has its source. To the west of Egypt is death. That is the endless desert. There the Egyptians have always buried their dead, who go, so it was said, to "meet Osiris in the west".

Egypt, in the words of its ancient people, is the body of Osiris. Abydos, his heart. The Delta, his head. The obscure regions beyond the cataracts were felt to be like the lower organism, impenetrable to human consciousness. After death, it was said, the soul must pass through fifteen stations, of which the twelfth corresponded to the cataracts. There the Nile God waited and beside him the crocodile-headed creature who guarded the passage into the realms beyond. The legend says that Osiris' body was torn into fourteen pieces and scattered abroad. Isis, his devoted wife, sought out the fragments and buried them where she found them, erecting a temple at each place. Historically, we know that the government of Egypt was originally divided into fourteen provinces. Every year the festival of the restoration of Osiris was accomplished by the procession of priests who passed, in the footsteps of Isis, from one temple to the other, finally culminating their journey at Abydos where the heart of Osiris was said to lie. Even in the geography of Egypt its mythology is interwoven. Everywhere the presence of Isis, Osiris and Horus can be felt, and they will become as familiar to the teacher preparing this period as the physical profile of the land itself. We will come to recognize in Osiris, as the ancient Egyptian did, the original, divine and kingly being of man who is torn to pieces in entering the world of the senses, and by his passions. In Isis, the Egyptian saw the picture of the human soul on earth, continuously longing and searching for its lost connection with the divine. Horus, their child, born after the death of Osiris, is the individual spirit of man, born out of suffering and isolation. Thus, in mythological pictures the ancient world spoke of the deeper truth which it recognized below the surface of ordinary experience.

And Greece? Everywhere sea and rocky hills. Valleys, isolated from one another, but often giving on the sea and thus connected with all the Mediterranean world. Hundreds of islands. The Greek was as naturally a mariner and merchant-traveller as the Egyptian was preserved from outside contact with the world. Greece faced east toward Persia and the ancient empires as well as north and west toward barbarian Europe. No wonder, therefore, that the culture whose task it was to be the transition from an ancient way of life and thought to that of the modern world should have sought out Greece for its home.

Contrast the olive tree of Greece and the granary of Egypt: the former, growing on poor soil, clinging to the rock, gray-green, gnarled, but yielding a poor man's harvest: oil, fruit, wood and shade—an independent, but frugal tree; and Egypt, whose ancient name was KAM, meaning the black land, the fruitful sediment of ages—no valleys—but one great horizontal, narrow plane. Every foot of ground was cultivated and all the land was laid out in geometrical design. Every peasant depended upon his neighbor for the flow of water through the irrigation ditches and all depended upon their overlord and he in turn upon the Pharaoh. Egypt—structurally, in the political and economic sense, a pyramid. Greece—an independence of separately centered communities.

In addition, let us compare two moments from the spiritual life of these two great cultures. What a different experience the Egyptian must have had when entering one of the vast temples bordering the Nile, from the Athenian who centuries later climbed the Acropolis to worship at the shrines of Zeus or Athene. Imagine the voyage down the Nile to Abydos or Karnak:—the ascent of the broad steps which led up from the river—the approach to the temple along the paved avenue where from both sides the impassive countenance of many sphinxes gazed down upon the traveller. Standing before the sphinx the Egyptian experienced the riddle of his own being. Proceeding between the rows of sphinxes he approached the obelisk and pylon whose massive walls were covered entirely with hieroglyphs. Passing beneath the heavy flat portal of the pylon, the traveller entered the temple's great court at whose farther end the ponderous forest of pillars, supporting the flat roof, stretched away into darkness. The slant light from the narrow opening below the central roof illuminated the vast columns whose colors must have worked strongly upon him. And every pillar was also a monumental tablet upon which was painted the sacred script telling of Osiris, Horus and Isis, and of the way of the soul through life and after death. The traveller who left the bright courtyard behind him in which the crowds thronged, entered the gathering twilight and deepening silence of the hall of pillars whose lotus bud and lotus flower capitals towered far above him. Beyond this, only the consecrated priest might go.

The innermost sanctuary was entirely cut off from the light of day. Its only illumination was the sacred flame which burned upon the altar. Here, in complete outer darkness, the Egyptian priest worshipped Osiris, the being of light, the same being who was sought by the soul after death. His realm was not a realm of darkness to the Egyptian, but one of light far brighter than the dazzling sun reflected upon the desert outside. The monumental record of the Egyptian conception of life after death, known to us today as the "Book of the Dead" was actually referred to originally as: "Chapters of the Coming Forth by Day"! In Egypt then, the human being left the world of outer, physical light in order to unite himself inwardly with the world of spiritual light. The mighty pyramids themselves are witnesses of this fact. The Great Pyramid of Khufu, for instance, which was built as a tomb and ceremonial chamber for the rites of the dead was known as "The Light".

Now let us go to ancient Athens. The temple of Athene is raised above the city and can be seen from far away. It is in the midst of nature and the wind and sunlight play through it, penetrating even into the presence of the goddess herself. All citizens are free to enter the temple; there are no hidden sanctuaries. Although the Parthenon is large it appears to have no heaviness in it: it is in perfect balance. In Egypt the triangular sides of the pyramid were perfect in their mathematical accuracy and immense in size and sheer weight. Their forms reflected the cosmic laws of astronomy in the mass of earthly substance. In the Greek temple the triangle is lifted from the earth and is freed from its heaviness. It is no longer merely a form of pure cosmic geometry but an expression of human artistic beauty. The pediment has become an architectural crown in which the free movements of the sculptured figures find measurement and order. The pillars of an Egyptian temple were superhuman in dimensions; the Greek columns are in perfect balance between heaven and earth. They stand like a beautifully proportioned human being—free, yet exactly suited to carry the weight required of them. The Egyptian statue also was more than human. The gaze was fixed in other than merely human focus. The inner attitude was one of listening. The body was constrained, the features impassive; the size immense. The effect upon the observer was one of awe—of a sense of mystery—a premonition of a world beyond the senses.

The Greek sculpture is ideal—but ideally human. It moves. Its proportions are the unspoiled proportions of the human body. It is the product of a world of beauty to be found only upon earth. The walls and columns of a Greek temple are not covered over with writing telling of another world. They speak the language of pure art. For the Greek, the temple was actually the dwelling place of the god. The divine had entered fully into the earth and was no longer, as in Egypt, to be sought in a sphere overshadowing the earth. The world beyond the senses had grown dim and gray. The earth and the human body, the life of art and of the mind, preoccupied the Greek. The ancient Egyptian could never have said: "Better to be a beggar in the land of the living than a king in the realm of the shades." To the Greek, however, it exactly expressed his feelings. The Egyptian still dreamed. The Greek was awake to life. It was the task of his philosophy to translate the dreaming world of the Egyptian wisdom into a language which could be grasped by the intellect. Plato, who was a student of the Egyptian mysteries, was one of the great leaders in this work. Aristotle, his pupil, was the father of modern science. Alexander the Great, Aristotle's pupil, carried the philosophy of Greece over all the ancient world. A new age was dawning for mankind.

If the teacher of history will awaken the dramatist within himself he will discover how the mass of historical detail begins to speak another language. Instead of incoherent sounds, words emerge which tell him of a pattern of reality hidden just below the surface of events. Even the present years can be understood against the perspective of world history. Each epoch has its task and its own struggle. If, in their history lessons, children can come to feel this inner movement of development from one age to the next they will gain confidence with which to face the tasks and struggles which await them in their own lives. If they feel that there is sense and meaning in history they will also come to see that their individual contributions, too, can not be meaningless.

(1960) —Henry Barnes

Biography In Education

We are all individuals. Occasionally we fiercely defend our individual rights and freedom as a unique entity—a centric being which we call "I." Often we feel imprisoned within the physical vessel we call a body—sometimes striving to protect itself from other bodies with a will and independence of their own. We can easily sense the meaning of Schweitzer's 'reverence for life.'

'I am the life that wills to live in the midst of other life which wills to live.' Yet as we set great store by our independence, so do we all possess a deep desire to transcend the personal and unite with the lives of other beings around us. We bear the polarities of independence and social need and desire. We are caught in, or suspended within, a dynamic tension between ourselves and our fellows about us. The personal and the self-transcendent are a rack we are hung upon by the very nature of our humanity. There is a deep desire in us to know and to love our fellows, in spite of our weaknesses, and the frailties of our companions. Here lie the real roots of our need for biography. We can glimpse for a moment or two the correspondences between us. We can measure and reaffirm the nature of our humanity—that we belong to it with every other person.

Out of the richness of the Hebrew testament come the words, "I will lift up mine eyes to the hills, from whence cometh my help . . . my help cometh from the powers that transcend me . . . ," but also these words help suggest to me a way to see biography—the hills we often lift our eyes to could easily dissolve in the mists of our imagination, to become the great men and women who have graced the earth in the march of evolving consciousness. There are so many such hills to which we can lift our gaze.

We can derive great strength from these mountains of success, travail and pain, and strength of purpose. Like us they have toiled to fashion their destiny and to attain their goals. Olympian beings they may seem, yet we search to disclose their humanity, their failings and their virtues. They were human too and they were our brothers. They have gone before, and thus can help us find our way over the tortuous terrain we all have to negotiate. Through them, too, we reaffirm the nobility of man. We can value the purpose of pain and learn from those who have transmuted suffering into higher qualities and enrichment of being.

Biography is one vital dimension of education. In the first school year, no biographies are given. The wisdom of the fairy tales is a supra-personal picture of all beings and all kingdoms of nature and heaven. An archetypal biography is revealed in the fairy tales—a picture of pre-birth, life, death and rebirth, and the creative power and guidance in the universe. The struggle for direction and purpose is hidden behind these tales. The mission of the old travelling storyteller was not for amusement, nor entertainment, but one of instruction from the wisdom of the past.

In the second grade we will find the legends of the saints and animals. The stories of St. Francis, St. Jerome, St. Patrick, St. Valentine bring before the children feeling-filled pictures of the highest of men given to the service of the earth and their fellows. It is easy to recognize the root of a future ecology here, but the essence is the picture of a human as a near-perfected being in harmony with nature, with himself, and with others.

As the time of the awakening self-awareness approaches, the children feel themselves as separate beings or entities—they lose the world of fairy tales and fables, but gain a rich emotional expansion. Yet the path of isolation continues and deepens as they contract more and more into centric beings within their own self-awareness. Thus, the role of biography becomes ever more vital, to unite them with their humankind. The biographies given are not vague and haphazard, leaping hither and thither through the centuries, but as far as possible they are related to the historical epoch of the particular grade. The third-graders, for example, take part in the colossal lives of the patriarchs of the Old Testament and the struggle for self-identity and knowledge of good and evil.

The fourth-graders meet the Norse legends, simply teeming with magnificently proportioned biographies that represent, as it were, a personification of all the faculties within emergent man and all the powers within the cosmos.

In the fifth grade, we reach the beginning of a historical consciousness, and pass on from the Ancient Indian, Persian, Egyptian, to Greek legends and history. Great beings speak out of these times to contribute to the waiting, open souls of the children, strengthening the inner life, giving direction and guidance deep below the threshold of waking consciousness. In the fifth grade the Greek spirit will again emerge to speak in her inimitable rhythm of the poetry, drama, beauty and courage of her sons.

As the sixth-graders encounter the Roman world, biography will give them a deep insight into the Roman manner of life. This will not be a brief excursion into a history of dates and facts, but a penetration into the hearts and minds of the citizens and luminaries of Rome and her world. History will not be "one damned thing after another" or "a nightmare from which I am trying to awake" (James Joyce, *Ulysses*) but the emergence of a conscious humanity through meeting resistance and travail—a mirror of the individual path.

As the grades advance and the student approaches puberty, the value of biography intensifies. Remember that the Waldorf schools perceive puberty to be far more extensive than a mere sexual maturity. Of course, the physical changes are an important consideration, but they are the outcome of a greater process, the descent to the earth in more ways than one. Adolescents are deeply aware of themselves as separate entities, confused by and sensitive to a host of new feelings and to the nature of their physical changes. They are concerned with who they are and where they should go. This is the first time that they really sense what it is to be human—as an individual. The sense of loss, the withdrawal and sensitivity met with at the approach of puberty is another step in self-awareness. As the earthly physical development has reached a particular point, so the age of idealism and hero-worship arises. The young people are deeply concerned with the nature of life and human values. Here then is the gift of the biography. Men and women worthy of their esteem can speak to them from the past.

The struggle to live and grow will be demonstrated in a thousand ways in the incessant striving for self-development, in the failings and hypocrisies of men and in their virtues. As the ray of destiny penetrates the prism of life, it is manifest in a colorful spectrum which will absorb and intrigue the young soul. All this is the food they need at this time. Men of courage, the intrepid explorers, will show themselves and men and women of compassion and idealism; myriads of qualities will reveal themselves through biography. Madame Curie, Galileo, Schweitzer, Braille, Lincoln, Einstein, Nobel, Helen Keller, Michelangelo, Raphael and Leonardo, Beethoven will speak to them. There will be a balance of good and bad, the enlightened and the misguided, the tyrants and the saints, those who sacrificed their lives for human liberty, those who seek to heal and those who strive to understand. All the fruits of history can be brought to our students. They will recognize the humanity in everyone and feel it stir in their souls. They sense the nobility of the spirit of man—how they seek, how they lose the path, how they climb the heights. The young soul will respect this insight into the human life-span and will be touched by the gentleness of Emerson, the humility of St. Francis, the brilliant failures of Leonardo, the singleness of purpose of Columbus, the resilience of Madame Curie, the crushing burdens of Beethoven, the equanimity of Buddha, the invincibility of Moses, the refined love of Elizabeth Barrett-Browning, the idealism and sacrifice of Martin Luther King, the soul-searching of Augustine or of Tolstoy, and the hate of Hitler, the ruthlessness of Rhodes, and the selflessness of Gandhi.

All these dangers, enigmas and qualities are within our students as potential. The tempest and the wilderness that faced those who have passed will come to face those who have to come. Yet we will encourage them to see beyond the obscuring mists and impeding marshes to the clear sun-covered peaks that are the finest heights of human achievement.

Biography possesses remedial qualities, too, for we can bring a great life to bear on the particular problems of a child. This can be related to and guided by the temperaments. The choleric will grasp for the leaders of men, their nobility of purpose, or will perceive the narrow greed that drove them on to self-destruction. The melancholic will drink deep the draught of lives dedicated to the overcoming of suffering, or those who sink beneath the weighty burden of life. The sanguine will be delighted by a fast-changing life, the eagerness, the vitality and vivacity of a many-faceted purpose, or the dissipation by the temptations that lie along the way. The phlegmatic will be encouraged by those who stand resolute and firm, upholding their tasks in spite of the floods and storms that inundate them, or recognize those who fail to act when the time is ripe—monuments to lost opportunity.

The intuitive teacher can find in Biography an endless creative source of healing and balance that can be directed to the needs of his pupils. Many reflect on a grand scale the basic problems of a particular student. Intuitively, one can sense that both a particular student and a particular biography reveal the same fundamental problems, thus the biography can be given as a story, as drama, or in artistic form, in poetry or music. In the middle and lower grades the biography must not be explained, for deep in the metabolism of the soul there will be a recognition. In adolescence or college, biography can be used as another, more conscious medium by the counsellor.

Biography is a perpetual source of tolerance and compassion for our vices and virtues. It can stimulate a feeling that beneath the integuments of creed, color and nationality, of success and failure, we are all brothers and sisters, for we all must travel the road between birth and death. Herein lies one of the great roots of an enlightened humanism; a foundation for humanity ... and as the light of a higher awareness dawns within young persons, they will sense the common thread woven into the complex tapestry of us all—and the creative, directional spirit within themselves and their fellow travelers.

(1970) —William Bryant

A Creative Approach to Foreign Languages For Waldorf Teachers
With Special Reference to French and German

The teaching of foreign languages plays an essential part in the Waldorf curriculum. In the original Waldorf School, Rudolf Steiner intended children to be exposed to two contrasting foreign languages, three times a week, from the first through the 12th grade. The learning of a foreign language greatly depends on imitative musical abilities. Although these abilities are somewhat ebbing from the change of teeth onwards, the language teacher can still make use of them in a most creative way. Much will depend for the future mastery of the language on whether in these early grades the children can be submerged in the living atmosphere of the spoken word. The classroom—whether French, Spanish, Russian, German or any other language is taught—should become for the duration of every language lesson a part of that particular country. Ideally, not a word of the native language should be spoken there. The children will be greeted in French (for instance): "Bonjour, mes enfants. Comment allez vous aujourd'hui?" The class replies, "Tres bien, merci. Et vous?" Out of this dialogue, we might come to speak about the weather. "Regardez, il fait beau aujourd'hui. Le soleil brille." . . . "Oh, quel temps! Il ne fait que pleuvoir." After this lively dialogue the class in chorus will practice a number of pronunciation exercises. First, two or three are introduced, and then, little by little, through the weeks and the months, a whole repertoire is built up. It might take three or four minutes to recite these in chorus and individually. The class will also stand up and appropriate movements can be introduced.

"Ton thé t'a-t-il ôté ta toux?"

"Tue ta toux avant que ta toux te tue."

"Bon Papa, ne bats pas beau Paul."—and many others.

The importance, though many of these are humorous, does not lie in the meaning but in the tongue-twisting ability of learning to cope with the sounds. And then, the class will be led into the recitation of a poem. Here again, the musicality and the mood is stressed. Great poetry is chosen rather than the jingles written specially for children. Already at an early age, children can be introduced to the genius of fine poetry: Ronsard, Charles d'Orleans, LaFontaine, Victor Hugo, Lamartine, Leconte de Lisle, Theophile Gautier, and others. Gradually, a rich repertoire of poetry which is learnt by heart solely out of the oral element can be built up. It is an invaluable treasure in later life, and more than anything else it develops a sensitive appreciation for the language. As an example, we quote a poem by Charles d'Orleans (1391-1465), "Rondeau", which he wrote during his long captivity of more than 20 years in the gloomy fortress of the Tower of London and where he recalls nostalgically the sweet beginnings of spring in his beloved France:

" Le temps a laissé son manteau
De vent, de froidure et de pluie,
Et s'est vêtu de broderie
De soleil luisant, clair et beau.
 Il n'y a bête, ni oiseau,
Qu'en son jargon ne chante ou crie:
Le temps a laissé son manteau
De vent, de froidure et de pluie.
Rivière, fontaine et ruisseau
Portent en livrée jolie
Gouttes d'argent, d'orfèvrerie,
Chacun s'habille de nouveau.
Le temps a laissé son manteau."

In dealing with such a poem one will of course not stress either difficulties of vocabulary or points of grammar. That would be totally inartistic. The children, out of the mood of the language, will gain a sufficient understanding through the spoken word. No translation need be given. But by way of a vivid introduction in French and the use of the blackboard, the general meaning can readily be conveyed. One could ask the students briefly to retell in English the substance of the introduction that the teacher has given. In working with a poem, it is important that the teacher himself/herself has memorized it well and can recite it with enthusiasm. One might only spend about five to ten minutes each lesson on the recitation of poetry, taking a few lines at a time, repeating, continuing the process from one lesson to the next until the poem is known in chorus by the whole class and individually by each child.

The Early Grades

From the first to the third grade, nothing is written and it should be stressed that all the work is done orally. One would proceed in a similar way in German or Spanish or any other language. During the remaining part of the lesson in these early grades, a great deal can be done by way of introducing the children to the seasons, to day and night, the kingdoms of nature: rock, plant, animal; the parts of the body, telling the time, the course of the day with its many activities. These can be mimed and acted: we are asleep, we wake up, we open our eyes, we jump out of bed, we wash ourselves, we dress, we have breakfast with the family; what do we eat? what do we wear? how do we go to school? etc. One might also bring a suitcase and unpack various items that one takes with one on a journey. Shopping, telling the time, and a host of other daily activities in the third grade, when the students have a building and farming block, can thus appropriately be woven into the foreign language teaching. The main activity of the lesson should certainly consist of practicing the language by way of speaking, reciting, singing, games, etc.—but also by creating moments when the children listen to a story that the teacher tells. The singing of folk songs and rhythmic acting songs accompanied by gestures can also play a major part in these lessons.

The same holds true for German as it does for French or other foreign language: only the finest poetry is chosen. What a joy and enrichment for children to be introduced as early as the age of six or seven to masterpieces by Goethe, Schiller, Uhland, Ruckert, Morgenstern. Great poets are the creators of language and embody the genius of their people, often with simplest, childlike potency.

Gefunden

Ich ging im Walde
So für mich hin,
Und nichts zu suchen,
Das war mein Sinn.

Im Schatten sah ich
Ein Blümchen stehn,
Wie Sterne leuchtend,
Wie Äuglein schön.

Ich wollt' es brechen,
Da sagt' es fein:
Soll ich zum Welken
Gebrochen sein?

Ich grub's mit allen
Den Würzlein aus,
Zum Garten trug ich's
Am hübschen Haus.

Und pflanzt' es wieder
Am stillen Ort;
Nun zweigt es immer
Und blüht so fort.

Goethe

The learning of foreign languages is highly effective and stimulating only to the extent that the teacher is able to bring considerable diversity to the lesson, yet never tires of repeating the form he has established. There should be much variety between standing up and sitting down, moving the desks to the side, creating a circle and again re-forming the setting of the classroom, and then again spending time listening quietly. Thus, the active and passive elements of the language receive their full due. It is obvious that in the first grades, as indeed later on, the children understand more than they can actually reproduce or express correctly. Great care should be given to beautiful and correct pronunciation; slovenliness should not be allowed to creep in.

The Middle Grades

In the fourth, fifth and sixth grades, we enter into a new phase. Gradually we can now begin to write down some of the poems, stories and dialogues acquired in the repertoire of the first three grades: it is essentially the task of the middle years to learn to read the foreign language by way of writing, to be able to do simple dictations and to write answers to questions that have first been dealt with orally in a living way. Now gradually the structure of grammar has to be brought in, starting with the verb (the doing word). Conjugations can now be learnt rhythmically by heart: Je suis, tu es, il est—clap, clap! Nous sommes, vous etes, ils sont—clap, clap! ... Ich bin, du bist, er ist—clap, clap! Wir sind, ihr seid, sie sind—clap, clap! ... with clapping, stamping, and appropriate movements. Out of the will nature of the language, the verb, one gradually develops the noun (the naming word), actually a more abstract activity, and then one weaves in adjective and adverb, which represent the feeling element of language. There is no need to teach grammar with the help of a text book. The children make their own. And over the years, it can be added to, unfolding from the simplest rules and exercises to the most complex ones. By and large, the grammatical points in the foreign languages will be taught about one year after they have been mastered in the native tongue; cooperation between the teachers can add greatly to bringing structure and form to this aspect of the work. Grammar should always be taught out of a lively relationship with the spoken word. It has an important place in giving a backbone to our understanding, but if it is brought too early or in an abstract way, it can do much to deaden our connection with the living word. There are unfortunately too many such instances today, resulting in a deep-seated dislike for foreign languages.

Much of what has been practiced by way of poetry, songs, pronunciation exercises, etc. will be continued in the middle grades, but now, in addition, the printed book will be introduced. At the end of the fourth grade, the students will have learnt to write the language beautifully and to read fluently and correctly from the board or from their own written books. A certain amount of copying is by no means a waste of time. It strengthens the spelling, and attention is thereby focused on a number of grammatical difficulties. We should always be ready to enjoy the oddities of the languages we are teaching, such as, "Un ver vert va vers un verre vert." . . . "Dirigent, Der Regent." Proverbs and idioms and the etymological derivation of words can now be brought in, adding spice and humor to the lessons, which progressively have also become more formal. An important place is now given to the telling and retelling of stories. One might start with legends and folk tales, and then in the fifth and sixth grades begin to add historical anecdotes. The stories are told in a lively, dramatic way by the teacher in the foreign language with the support of mime and blackboard, or even drawings that he or she might have made in advance. They should be relatively short, and after a first retelling, one can quickly ascertain whether the children have understood the main points. On a next occasion, the story will be told again, but now in a more elaborate form adding descriptions and dealing with points of vocabulary and idiomatic expression.

On the third occasion, the children will begin to retell the story and the teacher might write the first version on the board, guiding the process along. This can be worked on further by the children and can now be used in a variety of ways. It can become the object of a lesson in style, in grammar, in question and answer, or become the basis of a short dramatic scene that is now written down and acted out.

The telling and retelling of stories gains in importance after the sixth grade, and in the seventh, eighth and ninth grades it forms together with reading an essential part of the curriculum. The language teacher will be helped a great deal by considering the History and Geography blocks the children receive in their main lessons: sixth grade, Roman History, Middle Ages; seventh grade, Renaissance, Reformation; eighth grade, Revolution; ninth grade, Modern History. From the fifth or sixth grade onwards, the students should also become familiar with the geography of the country of which they are learning the language. But it should always be taught in that language. This could go hand in hand with the customs and habits of the different regions of France, for example, the Breton, the Alsatian, the people from the Provence and the Champagne, their folklore, their national costumes, their food, their legends, their industries and natural resources. This is the time to introduce the children to the French cheeses, the manufacture of wine and champagne, the perfumes of the Cote d'Azur, etc. Equally, one might bring examples of the various dialects in German: Bayerisch, Schwäbisch, Plattdeutsch. Again, if one were teaching Spanish, one would bring the regions of Spain to their attention in a lively way: the dances, the music, the cathedrals, the mentality of the Spaniard. But one would also deal with some representative Latin American countries, Mexico in particular. It should be noted that the audio-visual plays little part in Waldorf education, as so much more can be achieved through the lively creativity of the teacher in relation to the class.

High School

Treasures of the literature of the various languages in the form, to begin with, of poetry, then of the short story and later of the novel and the play will continue to be brought to the students. In the ninth, tenth, eleventh and twelfth grades, a careful literature curriculum should be established, but this of course cannot be maintained unless the basic skills of speaking, reading, writing, dictations and conversation have been well established in the earlier grades.

The following guidelines in connection with the high school may be useful. In the ninth grade, the youngsters are revolutionary, in the black and white phase of their development, swinging between the comic and the tragic. Here one can introduce the Sturm und Drang period of German literature: the young Schiller, the young Goethe. In French, one would deal with the French Revolution, and poems of Victor Hugo, André Chenier, appropriately related to the period. The short stories of Alfred de Vigny, Balzac, extracts from "Les Misérables" by Victor Hugo and "Le Comte de Monte-Cristo" by Alexandre Dumas, are most useful. The teaching of this grade should be accompanied by a dramatic note spiced with humor. It is also the time in which, as the intellectual ability of the student is now maturing, the grammar and structure of the language should be revised and firmly established.

In the tenth grade, romanticism plays a central part in the life of the teenager. One can now choose examples from lyricism and deal with aspects of the history of the language. Students are interested in etymology and the structure of language as long as it is brought in a lively fashion. They begin to enjoy more consciously the peculiarities of a language and the more one can bring comparative examples, also from Latin and Greek and possibly from some other language, the better it is.

The eleventh grade lends itself to the tackling of drama. No student of French should leave the high school without having experienced the difference between Racine, Corneille, and Moliere. Le Grand Siècle, for instance, can be used as a major project and brief excursions can be made into the earlier poetry with extracts from Chrétien de Troyes. In German literature one can contrast the drama of Goethe and Schiller, though a study of "Faust" would best be postponed until the twelfth grade. In addition, one can bring aspects of Wolfram von Eschenbach and other Minnesänger. It is during the eleventh grade that we deal in the main lesson with the story of Parsifal, the "pure fool," who fails to ask the crucial question because of his inner dullness. In this grade, the History of Music is introduced and the language teacher can be inspired to form his lesson so as to embody aspects of the general curriculum. For instance, he might deal with the biographies of great composers typical of a particular country: Rameau, Berlioz, Chopin, Debussy—for France; Bach, Mozart, Beethoven, Wagner—for Germany.

In the twelfth grade, special emphasis is given to the literature of today. Students of French should be introduced to Albert Camus, Antoine de Saint-Exupéry, Anouilh, Ionesco; and in German: Max Frisch, Dürenmatt, Wolfgang Borchert, Heinrich Böll, and others.

Furthermore, in the upper grades, students can be encouraged to present the fruits of their research in a particular area. Some might choose to speak about the political situation, the social conditions, aspects of government and the judicial system of a particular country. Others might choose to research more deeply the psychological traits comparing, for instance, the outlook of the Frenchman and German; others again might present vignettes of the crafts and industries of a particular region. Such projects are presented orally in the foreign language in front of the class, and then summarized in the form of an essay in French, or German, or Spanish, etc. by each student.

From the above considerations, it will already have become apparent that the teaching of foreign languages is not merely of pragmatic use. We endeavor to go far beyond a mere basic knowledge as is so often practiced today. What can be the significance of this more comprehensive approach? Doubtless, language is a means of communication between human beings, and it is perhaps one of the most important ones. It is also the gateway to understanding a particular folk which has its own genius, its own individuality, its own musicality, and expresses itself in countless manifestations of everyday life.

Language is born in the child by imitation during the first couple of years of childhood. First he moves, crawls, learns to walk, and then, out of gesture, speech is born as the mother tongue, and it is by way of speaking that the first glimmerings of thinking arise in the third year. Our whole way of thinking is, to begin with, determined by the language we speak, and it is well known that, once we start learning another language, we also begin to think differently. Every language has its own thought forms. Certain concepts and words are quite untranslatable from one language into another. The Frenchman says: J'ai raison (I have reason)—meaning I am right. The German says: Ich habe recht (literally, I have right)—when he means to say: I am right. The German has "Weltanschauung"; he is constantly striving for a total comprehensive view of the world. The Englishman prides himself on a "sense of humor", the Frenchman on "savoir vivre" (to know how to live, or, a way of living). The Frenchman uses "penser à" (to think at—which has an analytical connotation); the German "über etwas nachdenken" (literally, over something after-think)—the gesture of the word is more towards an all-comprising synthetic type of thinking; whereas the English "to think about" suggests that one goes around the subject viewing it from as many aspects as possible. Apart from such subtleties, let us take a few more common examples which seek to indicate that much is lost in translation. The word "tree"—especially if it is portrayed eurythmically—has quite a different sound gesture from the German word "Baum" or the French word "arbre." The sound gesture of "tree" might be said to emphasize the trunk, whereas "Baum" stresses rather the abundant foliage of, for example, a linden tree, while "arbre" might evoke the image of the typical slim poplars trembling in the wind that one finds along the roads of France.

More is lost in translation than is generally realized, and one of the tasks of teaching foreign languages in the Waldorf School is to recapture the genius of language which—as we master it gradually—can further the understanding of another nation, another way of thinking, another way of relating to life. Without such a bridge, much is lost that is enchanting and captivating, and also seeds of distrust and prejudice between peoples are sown. In addition, through the learning of two foreign languages from the early nursery rhymes and songs in kindergarten through the first to the twelfth grades, an ever-widening palette of inner colors is developed, quickening our understanding for our fellow human beings. Once we have learnt two foreign languages—given some aptitude and willing effort—the third, fourth and fifth come more readily, and again our range of inner sensitivity is expanded.

Each language can be compared to an instrument in an orchestra. It has its own genius but also its own limitations. English lends itself most appropriately to suggestion, to expressing things between the lines; it is full of innuendo, of the partial statement. German, on the other hand, with its pictorial-plastic character, is particularly well suited to philosophical discourse. It always strives to plumb the depths and soar to all-encompassing heights, whereas the French language is the immaculate instrument of precision, the rapier that pierces with a disciplined thrust.

Experience also shows that through the learning of a foreign language, we become more subtly aware of our mother tongue. We rediscover its own particular capacities of expression in speech, in prose and in poetry. From about the fourth grade on, very special attention will be paid to comparing proverbs and idiomatic expressions in the different languages. They are introduced little by little with appropriate examples: "Er hat einen Vogel"—he has a bird, meaning he is crazy. "Elle a une araignée au plafond"—she has a spider on the ceiling, meaning she has a bee in her bonnet. Much quaintness and humor can thus be introduced into the lessons. Also at this time, attention will be given to a beautiful musical way of speaking. Children should not only learn to speak correctly but also with due respect for the beauty and musicality of the language.

In conclusion, the profoundly social task for learning a foreign language should be stressed. Space does not allow me here to pay proper tribute to two of the early Waldorf teachers, Dr. Konrad Sandkühler and Dr. Herbert Hahn, who pioneered mightily the development of foreign language teaching in our schools, and who were living examples of the versatility, human outreach and social empathy which a genuine study of foreign languages must stimulate. Dr. Hahn, for instance, gave us, late in his life, his magnificent book "Vom Genius Europas" (unfortunately as yet untranslated), where he discusses the special contribution of the Italians, the Spaniards, the Portuguese, the French, the Dutch, the English, the Swedes, the Danes, the Norwegians, the Finnish, the Russians, and the Germans, by way of the uniqueness of their language, their folk, their geographical setting, and their way of life, each part of a total spectrum. The heightening of social awareness and understanding on earth through a living experience of foreign languages is an essential goal of language teaching. With Goethe, we can say, "What is more precious than gold?—The light.—What is more quickening than the light?—*Das Gespräch*" . . . conversation, that which takes place in speech between one human being and another.

Perhaps it may be said that the teacher of foreign languages in a Waldorf school is dedicating his efforts to the reenlivening of language so that a true sense of brotherhood may arise among human beings.

(1978) —René Querido

The Waldorf School Movement in North America

A Fiftieth Anniversary "letter" addressed to Waldorf School parents but really to all of us—from L. Francis Edmunds, founder and principal-emeritus of Emerson College, Forest Row, England.

Dear Parents,

I have been asked to write something for this anniversary number addressed specially to you. This I do very gladly in the form of a letter—rather rambling at first, as letters tend to be, but gathering to a point, I hope, at the end.

In 1969 I attended the 50th anniversary of the Waldorf School in Stuttgart, the mother school founded by Rudolf Steiner himself. In 1925 we celebrated the founding of Michael Hall, the first Waldorf school in an English-speaking country. Rudolf Steiner was still living and sent a message. And now we are celebrating in 1978 the 50th anniversary of the founding of the first Waldorf school in the New World, the Rudolf Steiner School, New York, and concurrently, of the inception of Waldorf education on the North American continent. I believe there are still some living to recall that very humble beginning in a private apartment home.

My own connection with the work in America dates back to 1952. It was from a captain's bridge that I first beheld the "cloud-capp'd" towers of Wall Street. There were then three elementary schools in all, the original Rudolf Steiner School, now finely set up in the house at 15 East 79th Street, the Waldorf School of Adelphi College (later University), and Kimberton Farms School* in Pennsylvania, the last two being the particular gifts of their former benefactors, the late Mr.

---

* Now the Waldorf School of Garden City and Kimberton Waldorf School.

and Mrs. Myrin. In addition, there was a brave, venturesome and unique residential high school at High Mowing in New Hampshire, the deed of Mrs. Beulah Emmet, which provided high school facilities for children coming up from the three elementary schools. That was all. It seemed slow growing for the space of a quarter of a century.

That autumn visit brought in—it may be said now—three invitations. The first came from Mr. Myrin offering me the leadership of Kimberton Farms School. The second came from the Board of Directors of the Rudolf Steiner School inviting me to bring my family to New York and to take over the charge of that school. The third came as a unanimous request from the teachers of the Rudolf Steiner School themselves to join them and help decide what the future of the school was to be, whether it should stay in New York, or whether in view of its slow growing, it would be best to move it elsewhere. Enquiries as to the latter had already been made. It was the third invitation, after consultation with my colleagues in England, that I eventually accepted, little imagining how much more was to follow.

There came a day in the summer of 1954, that is two years later, when six people assembled in the country house of the Barneses (at that time still the home of the poet Percy MacKaye). They were Christy and Henry Barnes, Dorothy and William Harrer (both long to be lovingly remembered), and Elizabeth and Francis Edmunds. Elizabeth was shortly to return to England; Francis, with his work permit procured, planned to stay for several months. He naturally asked what work program was envisaged for him. To this Dorothy replied: "We have no program. We wanted you to come, to be with us, and then to see what happened." Elizabeth looked her surprise. Was this sufficient reason for tearing oneself out of a heavily loaded program in Britain?

But that is how it was. During the next eight years I was to become a kind of recurring minor event at the New York Income Tax Department each time it was a case of returning home.

Well, then, what *did* happen?

At the school, when the new year was to begin, I found there had been real changes. The Board of Directors had all resigned, and the teachers now had the full direction of the school. They had been very busy painting and decorating the building from top to bottom, so that it simply shone; and so did the teachers, too, in eager anticipation of a hoped-for new era in which, for the first time, they could feel free.

I had met American children, mostly adolescents, during two years at the International School in Geneva—at that time half of the school was American. I had taught them, gone wandering through the countryside with them, produced them in plays, even in a Gilbert and Sullivan short opera, so I had come to know them very well. Now I was to meet American children on the spot. There, in Manhattan, one of the first main lessons I gave was on the Knights of King Arthur. That gave evident proof of how powerfully a young child can live in the pictures offered him. They became veritable twelve-year-old knights, and the young maidens in the class were not to be outvied in courtly matters and manners. There was a mother who wondered what had happened to her Billy—he now jumped up to open the door for her every time she got up to leave the room! We quickly became an all-around Round Table, the parents joining in as best they could, at least in spirit. The response of children just a year or two older to a scene from Shakespeare was to me quite remarkable. And there were parents who seemed really to know what the education was about. As the weeks went by, it became less and less possible for the school to be moved elsewhere. What was the next step?

Not without trepidation the parents were informed that the school was ready to carry the then eighth grade forward to a ninth grade. The announcement fell flat. "No good at all," said the parents. So far as they were concerned, it was to be a full twelve-grade Waldorf School or had better stop as it was. But they knew very well it could not stay as it was for another twenty-five years. The resolve just had to be made to carry forward to a full high school. But where, for the building was full chock-a-block already, and how to set about it, and with what resources, for there *were none*? All felt the challenge, teachers, parents, the children old enough to understand, friends of the school—all!

Then came a miracle. Just around the corner, a building, 15 East 78th Street, formerly the Walt Whitman school, stood empty and waiting and not yet on the open market. It even had a large statue in it of Walt Whitman himself—what could be more propitious? Money, yes money . . . but it *must* be found. Every one worked. The slogan was, "Go out and beg, but face to face!" There was an adult barometer marked out on a hundred-dollar scale, and beside it a children barometer with a dollar scale, and at one point the children were gleefully winning! What were the poor parents to do but swallow and prepare to be poorer?

In short, the needed capital was found. The building was bought. The ninth grade was established, and a further grade was to be added year by year. An anecdote is worth recording. A girl had come in new to the high school. Her father asked her if she liked the school. "Yes, I do." He asked if she was going to stay. "Yes, until I am twenty-one, for you see, at this school they add a new grade every year." And thus it was that the first Waldorf school in America was brought to completion, not through major donations but by a united effort with the conviction that it had to be.

In the second twenty-five years of the fifty, things moved more rapidly, indeed, with an increasing tempo down to to-day. Within a year the Waldorf School at Garden City also reached the twelfth grade, and Kimberton Farms School, a few years later. Then Highland Hall in Los Angeles was born and then the Sacramento School (through the initiative of the late Dr. von Baravalle) and then the Green Meadow School began stirring and the Toronto School and later the Detroit School and the Mohala Pua School in Hawaii and the Vancouver School; and then came Pine Hill School with a school bridge formed between it and High Mowing School so that, in a novel way, all the twelve grades are covered; the Washington Waldorf School came on the scene; and, more recently, Hawthorne Valley School, the Denver School, and Summerfield School; and now there is a regular spate of young schools growing up in northern California and elsewhere. And yet, this is not enough—for the size of America, it is not enough.

But also, since Emerson College in Sussex began in 1962, several centers for training Waldorf teachers have come into being in America itself, and more are likely to follow; many more teachers, well qualified in Waldorf methods, are needed. Perhaps the bare term 'method' is misleading. Waldorf education is not just theory and applied method—it is vibrant with life potentials for the great needs of our time.

The moral of this tale is that imagination promotes enterprise and leads to results. The imagination we speak of is one to fire hearts, and the results we strive for are to live on creatively and fruitfully in the destinies of our children.

We live at a moment in history when, due to the immense strides of modern technology, the world is clamped into a forced oneness. Even a slight disturbance at any one point is immediately communicated throughout the globe, a kind of evidence that humanity, in the truest sense, is intended to be a great, a many-membered, a vastly differentiated, and yet a single organism. It is for this the greatest in humanity have lived and died. We cannot hope to survive in any other way. Yet never has there been so much strife, never so many seemingly irreconcilable warring factions at all levels and in all domains, racial, political, ideological, national, economic, down to the disruptive influences in the intimacies of private and personal life. And hovering over all this seething turmoil amounting to chaos is the ever-present threat today of large-scale annihilation on this planet of man and all forms of existing life, a potential for destruction which so far surpasses the horrors of Hiroshima that the mind simply cannot grasp it. The instinct is to try not to believe it.

In like measure, therefore, springing from the inmost depths of human nature, there must arise a counter-force, a moral power unprecedented, to create a new balance in the affairs of life, a new fealty between human being and human being the world over, transcending all dividing influences proceeding from motives of hate. Instead of the sins of the fathers being visited upon their children to the second and third generation, may the blessings of enlightened parents flow to their children to strengthen them and the generations after.

I wish to summarize in a few sentences what is basic to all of us in this work whether as parents or as teachers.

Let us recall the faith of the little child in his unquestioning imitation of the adult, and let the adult receive this trust with an equal measure of veneration for the child and with a quality of love that is free from sentimentality and possessiveness.

Let us perceive in the elementary years how our children hunger not only for the material of outer bread but for the heroic stuff of human striving and endurance, the spiritual substance they need to acquire fortitude of soul. Let us, out of our protective care, find and bring them the bread, the moral sustenance they seek.

Let us recognize in our youth the idealism that is truly native to them, the idealism that by its very nature must long to reach beyond the set conditions as given, to new dimensions of enterprise and progress, to new horizons of the future—an idealism which today can so easily be undermined and destroyed—and let us meet our young people, whose lives we know are beset with perils, with enthusiasm born of our own vision, bringing courage for the future. Let us not as adults be defeated by the negatives that threaten to engulf us all.

Let us as parents and as teachers learn to see ever more clearly how Waldorf education carries in it the seed forces for healthy, meaningful living in practical undertakings, in social relationships, in moral integrity in the initiatives undertaken.

The Waldorf movement with its more than 160 schools spread through many lands wills to grow further. There was a time when pioneering teachers sought supporting parents. Today as often as not, it is pioneering parents who are calling out for the right teachers. This is an education never intended just for the few. What it can offer belongs to *all* children. We need more and more pioneering parents as well as pioneering teachers, parents who are not only sympathetic but who make themselves articulate for an education not only for their own children but for the generation to which their children belong. We stand before the awe-inspiring question of what that generation, and the generation after them, may have to be facing in fifty years' time. Let us be grateful for the degree of cultural freedom in this matter of education we may still enjoy—for that freedom is by no means everywhere. Let us as parents as well as teachers utilize the freedom that is still granted to us.

(1978) Francis Edmunds

Acknowledgments

As former editor of "Education as an Art," following Christy Barnes, my thanks went many years ago to the busy teachers who sent in the articles you find in this volume, written in time snatched on weekends, on holidays, or when the evening preparation had been done.

This year again they responded cheerfully to my request for birth dates and life descriptions. Is it not an inspiring list of courageous pioneers? What pictures flash into our minds when we read "taught 37 years in the New York school" or "founded the first school in the State of . . ."! Take note of the many who have entered the spiritual world and may still be guiding stars to "their children".

Thanks to those, too, who helped in so many ways to put these two volumes together: Gerald Karnow, M.D., editor and publisher, Susanne Berlin, Eleanor Chandler, Lisl Franceschelli, Dr. Manfred Leist (Bund der Freien Waldorfschulen, Stuttgart), Marcie Winston, Maryann Perlman, Walter Teutsch. And special thanks to all those English, Dutch, German, Swiss, and American children who brought their bright eyes and enthusiastic hearts to the teachers they loved.

Ruth Pusch

Biographies

CHRISTY BARNES ("Caterpillar Capacities: An Address to the Graduating Class")

(b. 1909) Class teacher, later high school English teacher at the Rudolf Steiner School, N.Y.C.; created and was advisor for award-winning literary annual there. Former editor of "Education as an Art" (See Introduction to this volume) and "Journal for Anthroposophy". Speech artist, speech teacher, poet, lecturer. Editor and manager of the Adonis Press.

HENRY BARNES ("History Teaching, a Dramatic Art"; "Some Characteristics of Steiner Education")

(b. 1912) For 35 years class teacher, history teacher, and chairman of the faculty at the Rudolf Steiner School, N.Y.C. Co-founder of the Rudolf Steiner Educational and Farming Association, Harlemville, N.Y. Adviser for many Waldorf schools. General Secretary and member of the Council of the Anthroposophical Society in America. Lecturer and author.

GERHARD BEDDING ("The Chladni Plate")

(b. 1929) Served as a Waldorf class teacher for 26 years, most of this time at the Garden City school. Has been a science writer and instructor in science education. Is now working for Camp Glenbrook.

WILLIAM BRYANT ("Biography in Education")

(b. 1933) Has marked the end of his 33rd year of teaching in Waldorf schools, from South Africa to Sacramento, by graduating in June 1990 his eighth grade class at the Morningstar Waldorf School in Gig Harbor, Washington.

RUDOLF COPPLE (Translator, "Drawing: From First Grade to High School")

(b. 1908) Born in Germany; educated in France. Taught eurythmy at Kimberton Waldorf School; French and German at Rudolf Steiner School, N.Y.C. and then class teacher there for 16 years. Pioneered at Hawthorne Valley School, Harlemville, N.Y. After retirement has been adviser to various Waldorf schools.

STEPHEN EDELGLASS ("Modern Physics in the Waldorf High School")

(b. 1936) Taught physics and engineering at Cooper Union and the Stephens Institute of Technology. Is now physics and mathematics teacher at Green Meadow Waldorf School, Spring Valley, N.Y. Co-author with Hans Gebert, Georg Maier, John Davy of *Matter and Mind: Imaginative Participation in Science* (1992).

FRANCIS EDMUNDS ("Feeling in the Growing Child"/"The Human Skull"/"Letter to Parents")

(1902-1989) Taught for many years and served as faculty chairman at Michael Hall, England; teacher and adviser at Waldorf schools around the world. Lectured and started things in many countries. Founder and principal of Emerson College, Forest Row, England. Author of *Rudolf Steiner's Gift to Education; Anthroposophy as a Healing Force*.

KARL EGE ("The Drama of Sound")

(1899-1973) Appointed as class teacher by Rudolf Steiner at the original Waldorf school in Stuttgart, Germany; became also a free religion teacher there. In 1948 became science teacher at the New York City school; helped establish the high school. Adviser, teacher-training in other Waldorf schools. Co-founder of the Rudolf Steiner Education and Farming Association, Harlemville, N.Y.

AMOS FRANCESCHELLI ("Mathematics in the Classroom")

(b. 1911) Born in Italy. Pre-college education in Italy, Germany and Canada; B.A. University of Toronto; M.A. Harvard. Taught in private and public schools, then from 1953 for 24 years at the Rudolf Steiner School, N.Y.C. as mathematics teacher. Since retirement, occasional short courses to Waldorf teacher-trainees and contacts with math teachers in Waldorf schools in an advisory capacity.

CARL FROEBE ("Drawing: From First Grade to High School")

(1900-1967) Artist and painting teacher at the Rendsburg, Germany Waldorf School from 1950 until his death.

MARGARET FROHLICH ("Bookbinding in the High School")

(b. 1900) Born in Vienna, trained in architecture. Teacher of handwork, woodwork, form drawing, color theory at Kimberton Waldorf School 1948-1957. Taught handwork, bookbinding, History of Art, and History of Architecture at the Rudolf Steiner School, N.Y.C. 1957-1970. Since retirement has worked in teacher training across the country and in Canada, Mexico, and Colombia, as well as with teachers in established Waldorf schools. Translated Gerbert's *Education Through Art* and Richter's *Art and Human Consciousness*.

ERICH GABERT ("What is so Special about the Waldorf Schools?")

(1890-1968) Was the last teacher appointed by Rudolf Steiner to the faculty of the first Waldorf School in Stuttgart, Germany (1924). Class teacher and history teacher in the upper school. Edited valuable collection of helpful suggestions made by Rudolf Steiner for the teaching of history, literature, grammar, foreign languages, and religion in Waldorf schools. Author of *Educating the Adolescent: Discipline or Freedom?; The Motherly and Fatherly Roles in Education; Punishment in Self-Education and in the Education of the Child*.

JOHN F. GARDNER ("Grace at Meals: A Talk to the High School Students")

(b. 1912) Taught at the Rudolf Steiner School, N.Y.C. 1935-1937, with his wife Carol. Was called by Adelphi University in the late '40s to supervise the development of its fledgling Waldorf school in Garden City, N.Y. There he remained for 30 years, serving as Faculty chairman for 25. Founder and director of Adelphi's Waldorf Institute for Liberal Education. Succeeded Dr. Franz Winkler as president of the Myrin Institute for Adult Education. Author of *The Experience of Knowledge* (1975) and *Heralds of the American Spirit* (1991).

NANETTE GRIMM ("A High School Course in Child Study")

(b. 1925) Taught at all levels in the Rudolf Steiner School, N.Y.C. for 33 years: kindergarten, class teacher, high school biology and chemistry. Established the child study course in the twelfth grade and carried it for 13 years.

GLADYS BARNETT HAHN (Translator of many articles from the German)

(b. 1897) Taught kindergarten in the early years of the Rudolf Steiner School, N.Y.C. Curative eurythmist, teacher and director in the first work in America for the mentally handicapped that preceded the Camphill movement here. Taught school classes for staff children at Camphill Village, N.Y., the nucleus for what later became Hawthorne Valley School in Harlemville.

HERBERT HAHN ("At the Beginning")

(1890-1970) As a young man of 29, Dr. Hahn was invited to initiate a new kind of school, a forerunner of adult education, within the cigarette factory of Emil Molt in Stuttgart, Germany for the workmen. Lectures and discussions took place during the work hours as a gift of the management but also as the result of a strong wish for further education. It was out of this activity that the first thought of a school for the children of the factory workers developed, especially from worker-parents. Hahn was born in what is now Estonia, was a teacher in Russia and Holland and a military interpreter in both world wars. Lecturer and author of many books, including *Vom Genius Europas* and his autobiography (not yet translated). A book about religious instruction in the school was published in 1977 with the title *From the Wellsprings of the Soul*.

JEAN HAMSHAW ("Teaching Medieval Romances")

(b. 1917) Taught High School English in the Garden City Waldorf School 1956-1978 and also served as an administrative secretary under Faculty Chairman John Gardner.

DOROTHY JEFFREY HARRER ("Independence in Education"/ "A Class as a Community")

(1905 1977) Born in India, took up social work until, discovering Waldorf education, she became a class teacher at the Rudolf Steiner School, N.Y.C. and remained there 30 years until her retirement. Wrote many textbooks for Waldorf teachers (her own "curriculum planning"): *An English Manual, Math Lessons for the Elementary School Grades, Nature Ways*.

A.C. HARWOOD ("Study of Man")

(1898-1975) One of five teachers—four of them women—who founded the first Waldorf school in Great Britain, now Michael Hall in Sussex. Class teacher and then specialist in history, literature and classics; chairman of the College of Teachers for many years, chairman of the Anthroposophical Society in Great Britain for 40 years. Lectured in the United States; toured here with his wife Elizabeth, the eurythmist, for whom he recited. Author of many books on education and literature, among them *The Recovery of Man in Childhood, The Way of the Child, Shakespeare's Prophetic Mind*.

FREDERICK HIEBEL ("A First Approach to Mineralogy")

(1903-1989) Poet, dramatist, biographer, essayist; came from his native Vienna in the early '30s to the U.S. Taught in the Rudolf Steiner School, N.Y.C., Wagner College, Rutgers and Princeton. His field was German literature; he published important studies of Goethe and Novalis. Became in 1963 a member of the Vorstand of the General Anthroposophical Society in Dornach, Switzerland; edited the weekly, *Das Goetheanum;* author of *The Gospel of Hellas, Shakespeare and the Awakening of Modern Consciousness, Time of Decision with Rudolf Steiner,* and many others.

RUTH HOFRICHTER (Translator, "Linear Thinking")

(1896-1977) Born and educated in Germany, she was one of the first women to earn a doctorate from a German university. Professor of German Literature, then head of the German department at Vassar College. Her specialty was Goethe's *Faust*.

BETTY KANE
See Betty Staley

ERNST KATZ ("Of Machines and Men")

(b. 1913) Professor of physics (retired) at the University of Michigan; has lectured world-wide. Founder of the Rudolf Steiner Institute of the Great Lakes in Ann Arbor, associated with the Rudolf Steiner School of Ann Arbor. Dr. Katz is author of *About Your Relation to Rudolf Steiner*.

ELISABETH KLEIN ("Children's Quarrels")

(1901-1983) Helped to found the first Waldorf school in Dresden, Germany, in 1929; married the Christian Community priest Gerhard Klein. When the school was closed by the Nazis in 1941 (not to be opened again until the fall of the Berlin Wall), she became a prolific writer of children's books and articles about education for numerous magazines; especially concerned with the elementary grades in Waldorf schools. After World War II she became a class teacher at the school in Hanover and also taught science in the High School.

CHRISTOPH LINDENBERG ("Linear Thinking")

(b. 1930) Teacher of history, English, and social science at the Tubingen Waldorf School in Germany. Author of *Teaching History: Suggested Themes for the Curriculum in Waldorf Schools* and other books on education not yet translated, among them *Waldorfschulen: angstfrei lernen, selbstbewusst handeln*. Member of the Vorstand of the Bund der Freien Waldorfschulen in Stuttgart, Germany.

A.W. MANN ("The Value of Art for the Adolescent")

(1900-1986) Born in Poland, grew up in Germany. Brother of George Adams, the scientist. Invited to teach German at the New School in London, which later became Michael Hall in Sussex, Mann soon began to teach woodwork, drawing, singing, religion, history of art. His greatest subject all his life was art history; he lectured on it all over the world and in many schools. After 50 years at Michael Hall he lectured and taught at Emerson College.

JAMES PETERSON ("Waldorf Education and the Public Schools")

Has taught in public and private schools for 21 years. He is currently teaching kindergarten and first grade in Canyon, California. Author of *The Secret Life of Kids: An Exploration into their Psychic Senses*; lecturer at J.F. Kennedy University in Orinda.

HERMANN POPPELBAUM ("Principles and Growing Human Beings")

(1891-1979) Dr. Poppelbaum was Visiting Lecturer in Psychology and Anthropology at Alfred University during World War II; taught the sciences in English and American Waldorf schools. Lectured on Anthropology and Anthroposophy. Author of *Man and Animal; A New Zoology; New Light on Heredity and Evolution,* and others. Chairman of the General Anthroposophical Society in Dornach, Switzerland, for some years.

RUTH PUSCH (Translator; editor)

(b. 1907) With Marjorie Spock the first American eurythmists teaching and performing from 1930 on, with Lucy Neuscheller whom Rudolf Steiner had sent from Dornach seven years earlier. Married to Hans Pusch, actor, student of Marie Steiner, stage director; together they translated and edited Rudolf Steiner's *Four Mystery Dramas* and *Calendar of the Soul.* Ruth taught eurythmy, kindergarten, high school English and drama in various Waldorf schools, notably at the Rudolf Steiner School, N.Y.C. Editor of "Education as an Art" 1959-1978.

RENÉ QUERIDO ("A Creative Approach to Language Teaching")

(b. 1926) Born in Holland, educated in France, Belgium and at Michael Hall in England; science and mathematics degree from London. Began teaching at Michael Hall in 1949. Co-director of Threefold Center for Adult Education at Spring Valley, N.Y.; taught, founded, advised several Waldorf schools. Established teacher training and adult education at Rudolf Steiner College in Sacramento. Lecturer in many countries; author of *The Golden Age of Chartres, Questions and Answers on Reincarnation and Karma, Creativity in Education, The Mystery of the Holy Grail.* Member of the Council of the Anthroposophical Society in America.

SHIRLEY and BOB ROUTLEDGE ("It's Easy to Start a Waldorf School, But ...")

They were instrumental in getting the Toronto, Ontario Waldorf School started (see their article) and were many years active in it and in the school movement. Their longer article, "The Infancy of a Waldorf School" is still available.

MARJORIE SPOCK ("The Community Sense in Child and Adult")

(b. 1904) Has taught at the Dalton School, Ethical Culture School, Rudolf Steiner School, N.Y.C. and the Waldorf School of Garden City. Eurythmist, translator, author: *Teaching as a Lively Art; Eurythmy; Reflections on Community Building* and others. Biodynamic farmer in Maine.

BETTY KANE STALEY ("Wish, Wonder, and Surprise"/"The Challenge of Grades 7,8 and 9")

(b. 1938) Class teacher at Sacramento Waldorf School; helped start the High School there and has been teaching literature and history in the upper grades for 16 years. Involved in teacher training at Rudolf Steiner College, Sacramento. has given lectures and workshops on Waldorf education and parenting for the past 20 years. Author of *Between Form and Freedom: A Practical Guide to the Teenage Years*.

GEORG STARKE ("But Wickedness Has To Be In It, Too")

(1904-1982) Studied mathematics and philosophy; from 1930 active in curative education. Was one of the founders of the Rudolf Steiner School, Schloss Hamborn, Germany. After the war he was class teacher at Waldorf schools in Marburg, Frankfurt, Krefeld, and Pforzheim.

WOLFGANG WAGNER ("The Education of the Will in the Crafts Lesson")

Was a teacher after the war at the New School, Kings Langley, England, where he wrote the article on crafts. The school later changed its name to the Rudolf Steiner School, Kings Langley. His subsequent life and teaching are unknown.

Waldorf Schools in North America – 1993

CALIFORNIA:

Rudolf Steiner College, 9200 Fair Oaks Blvd.,
Fair Oaks, CA., 95628, 916-961-8727

Waldorf Institute of Southern California, 17100 Superior Street,
Northridge, CA., 91325, 818-349-1394

Pasadena Waldorf School, 209 E. Mariposa St.,
Altadena, CA., 91001-5133, 818-794-9564

Live Oak Waldorf School, P.O. Box 57,
Applegate, CA., 95703, 916-878-8720

Waldorf School of Mendocino County, 6280 Third Street P.O. Box 349,
Calpella, CA., 95418, 707-485-8719

Waldorf School Of Monterey, P.O. Box 221057,
Carmel, CA., 93922, 408-372-4677

Mariposa Waldorf School, P.O. Box 1210,
Cedar Ridge, CA., 95924, 916-272-8411

Davis Waldorf School, 3100 Sycamore Lane,
Davis, CA, 95616, 916-753-1651

East Bay Waldorf School, 1275 61st Street,
Emeryville, CA., 94608, 415-547-1842

Sacramento Waldorf School, 3750 Bannister Road,
Fair Oaks, CA., 95628, 916-961-3900

Waldorf Community School, 11792 Bushard Street,
Fountain Valley, CA, 92708, 714-963-3637

Sierra Waldorf School, 19234 Rawhide Road,
Jamestown, CA, 95327, 209-984-0454

Waldorf School of the Peninsula, 401 Rosita Avenue,
Los Altos, CA., 94022, 415-948-8433

Highland Hall School, 17100 Superior Street,
Northridge, CA., 91325, 818-349-1394

Cedar Springs Waldorf School, 6029 Gold Meadows Road,
Placerville, CA, 95667, 916-642-9903

Camellia Waldorf School, 5701 Freeport Blvd.,
Sacramento, CA, 95822, 916-427-5022

San Francisco Waldorf School, 2938 Washington St.,
San Francisco, CA., 94115, 415-931-2750

Marin Waldorf School, 755 Idylberry Dr.,
San Rafael, CA., 94903, 415-479-8190

Waldorf School of Santa Barbara, 2300 B Garden Street,
Santa Barbara, CA., 93105, 805-569-2558

Santa Cruz Waldorf School, 2190 Empire Grade,
Santa Cruz, CA., 95060, 408-425-0519

Santa Monica Waldorf School, 1512 Pearl Street,
Santa Monica, CA, 90405, 213-450-0349

Summerfield Waldorf School, 155 Willowside Ave.,
Santa Rosa, CA., 95401, 707-575-7194

Sonoma Valley Waldorf School, Box 2063,
Sonoma, CA, 95476, 707-996-0996

Waldorf School of San Diego, 3327 Kenora Drive,
Spring Valley, CA., 91977, 619-589-6404

COLORADO:

Aspen Waldorf School, PO Box 1563, Aspen, CO, 81612, 303-925-7938

Shining Mountain School, 987 Locust,
Boulder, CO., 80304, 303-444-7697

Denver Waldorf School, 735 East Florida,
Denver, CO., 80210, 303-777-0531

FLORIDA:

Gainesville Waldorf School, 921 SW Depot Ave.,
Gainesville, FL., 32601, 904-375-6291

GEORGIA:

The Children's Garden, 2089 Ponce de Leon Avenue,
Atlanta, GA, 30307, 404-371-9470

HAWAII:

Haleakala School, R.R. 2, Box 790, Kula, Maui, HI., 96790, 808-878-2511

Honolulu Waldorf School, 350 Ulua Street,
Honolulu, HI., 96821, 808-377-5471

Kauai Waldorf School, PO Box 818, Kilauea, HI, 96754, 808-828-1144

Malamalama School, SR 13031, Keaau, HI., 96749, 808-966-9901

Pali Uli School, Box 1338, Kealakekua, HI, 96750, 808-322-3316

ILLINOIS:

Chicago Waldorf School, 1651 West Diversey,
Chicago, IL., 60614, 312-327-0079

MAINE:

Ashwood School, RR 1, Box 4725,
 Lincolnville, ME., 04849, 207-236-8021

Merriconeag School, P.O. Box 336,
 So. Freeport, ME., 04078, 207-865-3900

MARYLAND:

Waldorf School Of Baltimore, 4701 Yellowwood Ave.,
 Baltimore, MD., 21209, 301-367-6808

Washington Waldorf School, 4800 Sangamore Road,
 Bethesda, MD., 20816, 301-229-6107

MASSACHUSETTS:

Cape Ann School, 668 Hale Street,
 Beverly Farms, MA., 01915, 508-927-8811

Beach Rose Waldorf School, 85 Cotuit Road,
 Bourne, MA., 02532-0912, 508-563-9016

Rudolf Steiner School of G. B., West Plain Road,R.D.1, Box37B,
 Great Barrington, MA., 01230, 413-528-4015

The Hartsbrook Waldorf School, 94 Bay Road,
 Hadley, MA., 01035, 413-586-1908

The Lexington Waldorf School, 739 Massachusetts Avenue,
 Lexington, MA., 02173, 617-863-1062

MICHIGAN:

Rudolf Steiner School of Ann Arbor, 2775 Newport Road,
 Ann Arbor, MI., 48103, 313-995-4141

Oakland Steiner School, 1050 East Square Lake Road,
 Bloomfield Hills, MI, 48304, 313-646-2540

Detroit Waldorf School, 2555 Burns Ave.,
 Detroit, MI., 48214, 313-822-0300

MINNESOTA:

City of Lakes Waldorf School, 3450 Irving Ave. South,
 Minneapolis, MN, 55408, 612-822-1092

Minnesota Waldorf School, 2129 Fairview Ave. North,
 Roseville, MN., 55113-5416, 612-636-6577

NEW HAMPSHIRE:

Monadnock Waldorf School, 98 South Lincoln Street,
 Keene, NH., 03431, 603-357-4442

Antioch Waldorf Teacher Training Program, Roxbury Street,
    Keene, NH., 03431, 603-357-3122

High Mowing School, Wilton, NH., 03086, 603-654-2391

Pine Hill Waldorf School, Wilton, NH., 03086, 603-654-6003

NEW JERSEY:

Waldorf School Of Princeton, 1062 Cherry Hill Rd. RD#3,
    Princeton, NJ., 08540, 609-466-1970

NEW MEXICO:

Santa Fe Waldorf School, Rt. 9, Box 50-B3,
    Santa Fe, NM., 87505, 505-983-9727

NEW YORK:

Waldorf Institute of Sunbridge College, 260 Hungry Hollow Road,
    Spring Valley, NY., 10977, 914-425-0055

Rudolf Steiner School, 15 East 79th Street,
    New York, NY., 10021, 212-535-2130

Green Meadow Waldorf School, Hungry Hollow Road,
    Spring Valley, NY., 10977, 914-356-2514

Waldorf School of Garden City, Cambridge Avenue,
    Garden City, NY., 11530, 516-742-3434

Hawthorne Valley School, R.D. 2, Harlemville,
    Ghent, NY., 12075, 518-672-7092

Waldorf School of the Finger Lakes, 855 Five Mile Drive,
    Ithaca, NY., 14850, 607-273-4088

Mountain Laurel Waldorf School, 304 Rt. 32N,
    New Paltz, NY., 12561, 914-255-9225

Spring Hill School, 62-66 York Ave,
    Saratoga Springs, NY., 12866, 518-584-7643

Aurora Waldorf School, 525 West Falls Road,
    West Falls, NY, 14170, 716-655-2029

NORTH CAROLINA:

Emerson Waldorf School, 6211 New Jericho Road,
    Chapel Hill, NC., 27516, 919-967-1858

OHIO.

Spring Garden School, 2141 Pickle Road,
    Akron, OH., 44312, 216-644-1160

Cincinnati Waldorf School, 5411 Moeller Ave,
    Norwood, OH., 45212, 513-531-5135

OREGON:

The Waldorf School, P.O. Box 3240,
Ashland, OR., 97520, 503-482-9825

Eugene Waldorf School, 1350 McLean Blvd.,
Eugene, OR., 97405, 503-683-6951

Portland Waldorf School, 109 NE 50th Ave.,
Portland, OR., 97213-2907, 503-245-1507

PENNSYLVANIA:

Kimberton Waldorf School, West Seven Star Road,
Kimberton, PA., 19442, 215-933-3635

Susquehanna Waldorf School, 15 West Walnut Street,
Marietta, PA, 17547, 717-426-4506

RHODE ISLAND:

Meadowbrook Waldorf School, P.O. Box 508,
W. Kingston, RI., 02892, 401-782-1312

TEXAS:

Austin Waldorf School, 8702 South View Road,
Austin, TX., 78737, 512-288-5942

VERMONT:

Lake Champlain Waldorf School, 27 Harbor Road,
Shelburne, VT., 05482, 802-985-2827

Green Mountain School, RR 1 Box 4885,
Wolcott, VT., 05680, 802-888-2828

VIRGINIA:

Crossroads Waldorf School, Route 3, Box 189,
Crozet, VA., 22932, 804-823-6800

WASHINGTON:

Whatcom Hills Waldorf School, 941 Austin Street,
Bellingham, WA., 98226, 206-733-3164

Whidbey Island Waldorf School, Box 469,
Clinton, WA., 98236, 206-321-5686

Olympia Waldorf School, P.O. Box 638,
East Olympia, WA, 98540, 206-493-0906

Seattle Waldorf School, 2728 N.E. 100th,
Seattle, WA., 98125, 206-524-5320

WISCONSIN:

Waldorf School of Milwaukee, 718 East Pleasant Street, Milwaukee, WI., 53202, 414-272-7727

Prairie Hill Waldorf School, N14 W29143 Silvernail Road, Pewaukee, WI, 53072, 414-691-8996

Pleasant Ridge Waldorf School, 321 East Decker, Viroqua, WI., 54665, 608-637-7828

CANADA:

Rudolf Steiner Centre, PO Box 18, Thornhill, Ontario, L3T 3N1, 416-764-7570, Adults

Calgary Waldorf School, 1915 36th Ave. S.W., Calgary, ALBERTA, T2T 2G6, 403-287-1868

Halton Waldorf School, 83 Campbellville Road E., Campbellville, ONTARIO, L0P 1B0, 416-854-0191

Aurora Rudolf Steiner School, 7211 - 96 A Avenue, Edmonton, ALBERTA, T6B 1B5, 403-469-2101

Sunrise Waldorf School, 4344 Peters Road, Duncan, B.C., V9L 4W4, 604-743-7253

London Waldorf School, 1697 Trafalgar Square, London, ONTARIO, N5W 1X2, 519-451-7971

Nelson Waldorf School, Box 165, Nelson, B.C., V1L 5P9, 604-352-6919

Ottawa Waldorf School, 10 Coral Avenue, Nepean, ONTARIO, K2E 5Z6, 613-226-7369

Vancouver Waldorf School, 2725 St. Christopher's Road, N. Vancouver, B.C., V7K 2B6, 604-985-7435

L'Ecole Rudolf Steiner de Montreal, 12050 Bois de Boulogne, Montreal, QUEBEC, H3M 2X9, 514-334-5291

Toronto Waldorf School, Box 220, 9100 Bathurst st., Thornhill, ONTARIO, L3T 3N3, 416-881-1611

Kelowna Waldorf School, Box 93, 429 Collett Road, Okanaga Mission, B.C., V0H 1S0, 604-764-4130

Alan Howard Waldorf School, 228 St. George Street, Toronto, ONTARIO, M5R 2N9, 416-975-1349

MEXICO:

Colegio Waldorf de Cuernavaca, Jesus H. Preciado 103 Col. San Anton, Cuernavaca, Morelos, Mexico, 7318-8576

Rudolf Steiner/Waldorf Schools World List
(as of February 1993)

ARGENTINA: Buenos Aires (2)

AUSTRALIA: Adelaide, Bangalow, Bowral, Cawongla, Dorrigo, Hazelbrook, Maitland, Melbourne (3), Mount Barker, Nedlands, Newcastle, Perth, Sydney (3), Thora, Victoria/Yarro, Weston Creek, Yarramundi.

AUSTRIA: Graz, Innsbruck, Klagenfurt, Salzburg, Vienna (3).

BELGIUM: Aalst, Affligem, Antwerp (4), Brasschaat, Brugge (2), Brussels, Eupen, Gent, Leuven, Lier, Overijse, Raeren, Spa, Turnhout, Wilrijt.

BRAZIL: Botucatu, Camanducaia, Florianopolis, Riberao Preto, Sao Paulo (3).

CZECH REPUBLIC: Prague

CHILE: Santiago (2)

COLOMBIA: Cali, Medellin.

DENMARK: Aalborg, Åarhus (2), Copenhagen (2), Esbjerg, Fredericia, Hjørring, Kvistgård, Merløse, Odense (2), Risskov, Silkeborg, Skanderborg, Vejle, Vordingborg.

ECUADOR: Quito (2)

EGYPT: Bilbeis

ESTONIA: Polvamaa, Rakvere, Tallinn, Tartu

FINLAND: Espoo, Helsinki (2), Jyväskylä, Kuopio, Lahti, Lappeenranta, Oulu, Pori, Rovaniemi, Sammatti, Seinäjoki, Tammisaari, Tampere, Turku, Vaasa, Vantaa.

FRANCE: Chatou (Paris), Colmar, Laboissiere, St. Faust de Haut (Pau), Saint Genis Laval, Saint-Menoux, Strasbourg (2), Troyes, Verrieres le Buisson.

GERMANY: Aachen, Augsburg, Bad Nauheim, Balingen, Benefeld, Bergisch Gladbach, Berlin (5), Bexbach, Bielefeld, Böblingen, Bochum,

Bonn, Braunschweig, Bremen (2), Chemnitz, Chiemgau, Coburg, Cologne, Cottbus, Darmstadt, Detmold, Dietzenbach, Dortmund (2), Dresden, Düsseldorf, Duisburg, Eckernförde, Elmshorn, Engelberg, Erftstadt-Liblar, Erlangen, Essen, Esslingen, Evinghausen, Filderstadt, Flensburg, Frankenthal, Frankfurt, Frankfurt/Oder, Freiburg (3), Friedrichstal, Gladbeck, Göppingen, Göttingen, Gütersloh, Haan-Gruiten, Hagen, Halle, Hamburg (7), Hamm, Hannover (2), Heidelberg, Heidenheim, Heilbronn, Hildesheim, Hof, Jena, Kakenstorf, Karlsruhe, Kassel, Kiel (4), Kleinmachnow, Krefeld, Leipzig, Lörrach, Loheland, Ludwigsburg, Lübeck, Lüneburg, Magdeburg, Mainz, Mannheim, Marburg, Minden, Mönchengladbach, Mülheim (2), Munich (4), Münster, Neumünster, Neuwied, Nuremberg, Nurtingen, Offenburg, Oldenburg, Otterberg, Ottersberg, Pforzheim, Potsdam, Remscheid, Rendsburg (2), Reutlingen, Saarbrücken, Schloss Hamborn, Schondorf, Schopfheim, Schwäbisch Gmünd, Schwäbish Hall, Siegen, Sindelfingen, Stade, St. Augustin, Stuttgart (3), Trier, Tübingen, Überlingen, Ulm (2), Vaihingen/Enz, Villingen-Schwenningen, Wahlwies, Wangen, Wanne-Eickel, Wattenscheid, Weimar, Werder, Wernstein, Wiehl, Wiesbaden, Witten (2), Wolfsburg, Würzburg, Wuppertal (2).

HOLLAND: Alkmaar (3), Almelo, Almere, Alphen, Amersfoort, Amstelveen, Amsterdam, Apeldoorn, Arnheim, Assen, Bergen (2), De Bilt, Den Bosch, Boxmeer, Breda (2), Brummen, Bussum, Delft, Deventer, Doetinchem, Dordrecht, Driebergen, Ede, Eindhoven (2), Emmen, Enschede, Gouda, s'Gravenhage (4), Groningen, The Hague, Den Helder, Haarlem (2), Harderwijk, Heerlen, Helmond, Hertogenbosch, Hillegom, Hilversum, Hoofddedorp, Hoorn, Krimpen/Ijssel, Leeuwarden, Leiden (3), Maastricht, Meppel, Middelburg (2), Nijmegen (3), Oldenzaal, Oosterhout, Oud Beijerland, Purmerend, Roermond, Roosendaal, Rotterdam (3) Sittard, Terneuzen, Den Burg Texel, Tiel, Tilberg, Uden, Utrecht, Venlo, Voorschoten, Wageningen, Winterswijk, Zaandam, Zeist (4), Zoetermeer, Zutphen (4), Zwolle.

HUNGARY: Budaörs, Budapest (2), Dunakeszi, Gödöllö, Györ, Solymar.

IRELAND: Cooleenbridge, Dublin

ISRAEL: Nazareth

ITALY: Albano, Bosentino, Meran, Milan, Oriago, Rome, Trieste.

JAPAN: Tokyo

KENYA: Nairobi

LIECHTENSTEIN: Schaan

LUXEMBOURG: Luxembourg

NEW ZEALAND: Auckland (2), Christchurch, Dunedin, Hastings, Tauranga, Wellington.

NORWAY: Alesund, As, Asker, Askim, Baerum, Bergen (2), Drammen, Fredrikstad, Gjovik/Toten, Haugesund, Hedemark, Hurum, Kristiansand, Lillehammer, Lorenskog, Moss, Nesoddtangen, Oslo (2), Ringerike, Stavanger, Tönsberg, Trondheim, Tromso.

PERU: Lima (2).

POLAND: Warsaw

PORTUGAL: Lagos

RUSSIA: Moscow, St. Petersburg

SLOVENIA: Ljubljana

SOUTH AFRICA: Alexandra, Cape Town (2), Durban, Johannesburg, Meadowlands, Natal, Pretoria.

SPAIN: Alicante, Madrid.

SWEDEN: Delsbo (2), Garpenberg, Göteborg, Höör, Järna (2), Kalmar, Kungälv, Linköping, Lund, Märsta, Norrköping, Nyköping, Örebro, Rörum, Stegehus, Söderköping, Stockholm (3), Täby, Umeå, Västerås.

SWITZERLAND: Aldiswil, Aesch, Arlesheim, Basel (4), Bern(2), Biel, Chur, Dornach, Geneva/Confignon, Glarisegg, Herisau, Ins, Kreuzlingen, Langenthal, Langnau, Lausanne, Lenzburg, Lugano, Lucerne, Marbach, Neuchâtel, Pratteln, Schaffhausen, Schuls-Tarasp, Solothurn, Spiez, St. Gallen, Wetzikon, Wil, Winterthur, Yverdun, Zug, Zurich (2).

UNITED KINGDOM: Aberdeen, Belfast, Botton, Brighton, Bristol, Canterbury, Dyfed, Edinburgh, Forest Row, Forres, Glasgow, Gloucester, Hereford, Ilkeston, Kings Langley, London (4), Oxford, Plymouth, Reading, Ringwood, St. Albans, Sheffield, Snowdonia, Stourbridge, Stroud (2), Totnes, Tunbridge Wells, York.

URUGUAY: Montevideo

BOOKS ON WALDORF EDUCATION

By Rudolf Steiner

The Child's Changing Consciousness
The Education of the Child in the Light of Anthroposophy
The Four Temperaments
Education as a Social Problem
Education and Modern Spiritual Life
The Child's Changing Consciousness
Human Values in Education
An Introduction to Waldorf Education
The Roots of Education
The Renewal of Education
Soul Economy and Waldorf Education
Deeper Insights into Education
Self-Education: Autobiographical Reflections
Balance in Teaching
Study of Man
Practical Advice for Teachers
Discussions with Teachers
Waldorf Education for Adolescence
The Kingdom of Childhood

By other authors

Aeppli, Willi: *Rudolf Steiner Education and the Developing Child*
A.W.S.N.A.: *Multiculturalism in Waldorf Education*
Baldwin, Rahima: *You Are Your Child's First Teacher*
Barnes, H..,Howard, A.,Davy, J.: *An Introduction to Waldorf Education*
Benians, John: *The Golden Years*
Britz-Crecelius, Heidi: *Children at Play: Preparation for Life*
Carlgren, Frans: *Education Towards Freedom*
Edmunds, Francis: *Rudolf Steiner Education*
Edmunds, Francis: *Renewing Education*
Gabert, Erich: *Educating the Adolescent: Discipline or Freedom*
Gardner, John F.: *The Experience of Knowledge*
Grunelius, Elisabeth: *Early Childhood Education*
Haller, Ingeborg: *How Children Play*

Harwood, A.C.: *The Recovery of Man in Childhood*
    The Way of a Child
Koepke, Hermann: *On the Threshold of Adolescence*
    Encountering the Self: Transformation and Destiny in the Ninth Year
Lievegoed, Bernard: *Phases of Childhood*
Mitchell, D./Masters, B.: *Rudolf Steiner Waldorf Education*
Piening, E./Lyons, N.: *Educating as an Art*
Querido, René: *Creativity in Education*
Richards, M.C.: *Toward Wholeness: Rudolf Steiner Education in America*
Schwartz, Eugene: *Rhythms and Turning Points in the Life of the Child*
Setzer, Valdemar: *Computers in Education*
Sleigh, Julian: *Thirteen to Nineteen: Discovering the Light*
Spock, Marjorie: *Teaching as a Lively Art*
Staley, Betty: *Between Form and Freedom*
Wilkinson, Roy: *Commonsense Schooling*
von Heydebrand, Caroline: *Childhood: A Study of the Growing Child*
    The Curriculum of the First Waldorf School

This is a short selection of books on Waldorf Education available at the Anthroposophic Press:
    Bells Pond Star Route
    Hudson, NY 12534
and
    Rudolf Steiner College Book Service
    9200 Fair Oaks Blvd.
    Fair Oaks, CA 95628
Ask for catalogs, also at:
    Mercury Press
    241 Hungry Hollow Road
    Spring Valley, NY 10977
Inquire at the Rudolf Steiner Library
    RD#2 Harlemville
    Ghent, NY 12075
concerning their services.

"Child and Man", a Journal for Rudolf Steiner Waldorf Education (2 copies per year), Subscriptions $9.60.
    At The Sprig, Ashdown Road, Forest Row,
    East Sussex RH 18 5 HP, England

Association of Waldorf Schools of North America

David Alsop, Chairman
3911 Bannister Road
Fair Oaks, CA 95628
(916) 961-0927

The Association is a not-for-profit organization whose purpose it is to support and encourage the work of all Waldorf schools in North America.

"Renewal: A Journal for Waldorf Education" is published twice a year for individual members and for affiliated schools of the Association of Waldorf Schools of North America. Individual membership is $30.

Contents of Waldorf Schools–Vol. I:
Kindergarten and Early Grades

I. IDEAS AND INSIGHTS

Introduction 1
Betty Staley
What Do We Mean by Education as an Art? 4
William Harrer
The First Waldorf School.. 5
Al Laney
Independent Teachers and Independent Schools 13
Henry Barnes
Too Much Like Work?.. 20
Marjorie Spock
Gratitude, Love, Responsibility 24
Gisela O'Neil
Activity in Education.. 32
Alan Howard
The Effect of Waldorf Education on Home Life 38
Ruth McArdle
Pressure and the Spirit of Play 45
John Gardner

II. THE WALDORF KINDERGARTEN

The Kindergarten in the Rudolf Steiner School.................... 55
Alice S. Jansen
On the Moral Education of Young Children......................... 62
Christoph Boy
Adventures in the Park 74
Lona Koch
Eurythmy Lessons for Children of Three to Seven............. 77
Margarethe Buehler
The Inner Meaning of Children's Diseases: Measles.......... 82
Wilhelm zur Linden
The Importance of Fairy Tales in a Rudolf Steiner School. 86
Frederick Hiebel

III. THE FIRST FIVE GRADES

The Role of the Class Teacher and Its Transformation 91
Irmgard Huersch
The Teaching of Writing 96
Eileen Hutchins
Feeling in the Growing Child 102
Francis Edmunds
Color in Childhood 109
Trude Amann
How Eurythmy Works in the Curriculum 112
Kari van Oordt
Children's Play 117
Rudolf Kischnick
Modelling as the Expression of the Child's Inner Being .. 120
Elisabeth Klein
Handwork in the Early Grades 125
Patricia Livingston
In Third Grade 128
Susanne Berlin
A Teacher Talks to Her Children 131
Virginia Paulsen
Beginning Bible Stories 135
Margaret Peckham
Man and Animal 139
William Harrer
Work with Underprivileged Children 145
Gisela O'Neil
The Perfection of the Human Hand Lies in
 its Imperfection 153
Martha Haebler
Multiplication Tables Can Be Interesting 160
William Harrer
First Lessons in Botany 166
Virginia F. Birdsall

IV. THE WHOLE SCHOOL

Imagination at Different Ages 175
               I. van Wettum
"Earth, Who Gives to Us..." 180
               Betty and Franklin Kane
Choral Recitation 187
               Christy Barnes
Acknowledgments 193
Biographies of the Authors and Translators 194

Index

A

abstractions, 144
acoustics, 22, 73, 76, 96
activity, inner, 44
adjective, 185
adolescence, 21, 27, 82, 88, 95, 106, 129, 133, 178
Adonis Press, 3
adverb, 185
air, 96
Alcott, Bronson, 85
Alexander the Great, 175
algebra, 88
alienation, 116
Amish, 40
analysis, 136
anthroposophy, 9, 37
Anthroposophy and Science, 142
ape, 123
Archai, 16
Archangels, 16
architectural forms, 58, 137
Aristotle, 175
arithmetic, 68
arm, 80
art history, 105, 129
artistic expression, 132
arts, 22, 40, 111
AWSNA, 221
Athens, 173
atom, 117, 137
audio-visual, 187

B

baby-sitting, 128
balance, 39
balance, educational, 125
Barnes, Christy, 2, 134, 194
Barnes, Henry, 29, 168, 194
Baumann, Paul, 12
Bedding, Gerhard, 76
Beethoven, 74, 119, 179

Bentley, W.A., 85
Bible, 83, 176
biography, 169, 176
biology, 26
birth, 16
births, three, 105
black and white drawing, 166
blessing, 151
Board of Directors, 195
bookbinding, 123
"book corners", 162
"books, good", 127, 133, 185
Bosch, 112
botany, 69, 88, 134
breast bones, 100
breathing, 15
Breughel, 113
Bruner, J. S., 37
Bryant, William, 175
buoyancy, 131
butterfly, 134

C

cafeteria, 151
calculators, 118
capital, 196
carpentry, 81
caterpillar, 137
chambered nautilus, 150
character, 121
child study, 126
child, nature of, 8, 19, 25, 72, 75, 79, 94, 99
"Child and Man", 14, 220
"reading the child", 127
Chladni plate, 76
choreography, 78
chorus, 181
Chrétien de Troyes, 141
Christ, 112, 131
circle, 146
Clark, Sonia Tamara, 2
class teacher, 30, 72, 96, 101

clockwork universe, 116
color, 156, 165
communication, 74, 190
community, 19, 67, 73
computers, 41, 118, 150
concentration, 163
contraction, expansion, 15
control, 43, 154
Copple, Rudolf, 167
countenance, 120
crafts lesson, 79
criticism, development of, 133
crystals, 92
cultural life, 45, 46
curriculum, 31, 60, 68, 83, 106, 116, 127, 132, 139

D

death, 16, 135
d'Orleans, Charles, 182
decadence, 109
democracy, 21
democratic ideals, 24
Demosthenes, 136
Devil, 94
dexterity, 125
diagonal hatching, 166
diamond, 93
dictations, 185
digestion, 152
divisivenes, 72, 136
dome, 121
drama, 189
drawing, 99, 156
Dürer, 106, 113

E

earth, 72
Edda, 103
Edelglass, Stephen, 116
Edmunds, Elizabeth , 194
Edmunds, Francis, 118, 193
Education as an Art, 1
educational philosophy, 27, 31, 40, 45
Education of the Child, The, 94
Ege, Karl, 73

ego, 109
egotism, 50
Egypt, 112, 170
Egyptian sculpture, 130, 174
eighth grade, 105, 166, 187
electron, 117
eleventh and twelfth grades, 123
eleventh grade, 117, 147, 189
Emerson, 78, 85, 138, 179
Emerson College, 197
Emmet, Beulah, 194
empathy, 41
Emperor Hadrian, 17
English lesson, 82
enthusiasm, 170
environment, 49, 152
ethical-Christian impulse, 99
etymology, 188
Euclid, 147
eurythmy, 22, 40, 61, 87, 127, 128
evil, 95, 98, 109, 137
expansion, contraction, 15

F

faculty of teachers, 29, 45
faculty chairman, 31
faculty meeting, 47
fairy tales, 127, 176
family, 20
Faust, 50, 189
feeling, 19, 81, 97, 110, 119, 122, 125, 132, 153
fifth grade, 69, 169, 177, 185
finances, 56, 196
first grade, 127, 156, 176
first to third grade, 183
"The Fisherman and his Wife", 83
food, 126, 152
form, 99, 110
form drawing, 127, 157, 165
formative life forces, 16, 105
fortitude of soul, 198
forward thinking, 48
fourth grade, 67, 99, 108, 177
fourth, fifth and sixth grades, 185
Franceschelli, Amos, 4, 142
freedom, 45, 62, 130, 199
French, 181

French Revolution, 111
friendship, 21
Froebe, Carl, 156
Frohlich, Margaret, 123
Frostig, Gwen, 86

G

Gabert, Erich, 8
Gardner, John F., 65, 151
gems, 92
genius of language, 191
geography, 72, 88, 102, 187
geology, 88
geometric forms, 81, 157
geometry, 143, 145
geometry, projective, 147
German, 181
Geyer, Reverend Johannes, 12
Ghirlandaio, 113
God, 83, 143
gods, 130
Goethe, 89, 184, 192
Goetheanum, 137
gold, 91
goodness, 131, 137
Grace at meals, 151
Grail knights, 141
grammar, 23, 185
granite, 88, 102
gratitude, 152
gravity, forces of, 133
Greece, 112, 170
Greek sculpture, 131, 174
Greek spirit, 177
Grimm, Nanette, 126
Grohman, Gerbert, 69
groups, 21, 101
Grünewald, 113

H

Hahn, Gladys, 10
Hahn, Herbert, 11, 192
Hamshaw, Jean, 139
hand, 79
handwork, 124
Harlemville Farm School, 128
harmony, 160

Harrer, Dorothy, 45, 67
Harrer, Dorothy and William, 194
Harwood, A.C., 14, 105, 115
Hawthorne, 85
Hawthorne Valley School, 128
head, 100, 118
healing forces, 114, 134, 180
health, 151
heart, 137
Hiebel, Frederick, 88
High Mowing, 194
high school, 107, 115, 123, 151, 188, 196
history, 108, 168
history of art, 105, 110
history of music, 189
Hofrichter, Ruth, 52
hotheads, 101
Howard, Alan, 4
Human and Cosmic Thought, 146
human being, 33, 121
human body, 75
human values, 152, 178
human voice, 78
humanistic, 73
humanity, 180, 197
Husemann, Dr. Frederick, 87

I

I.Q., 50
idealism, 141, 169, 178, 198
illnesses, 153
image, school, 57
imagination, 169, 197
imaginative thought, 149
imitation, 94, 127, 198
independence, 45
individual, 120, 138, 178
individualism, 20, 23
individuality, 138
industry, 35
Infancy of a Waldorf School, 59
initiative group, 55
infinity, 147, 149
instinct, 152
intellect, 174
intellectual, 125

intelligence, 51, 134
iron, 92, 103
Isis, Osiris, Horus, 171
Italy, 102

J

James, William, 25
Jenny, Hans, 77
Jones, Michael, 154
Jones, Sir William, 17
Joseph, 130
Journal for Anthroposophy, 3
Joyce, James, 178

K

Kalevala, 103
Kane, Betty, (See Staley)
Katz, Ernst, 36
Kimberton Waldorf School, 193
kindergarten teacher, 126
king, 91
King, Martin Luther Jr., 179
Kingdom of Childhood, 158
King Arthur, knights of, 195
Klein, Elisabeth, 99
knowledge, 99, 130
knowledge, three stages of, 142

L

Language teaching, 181
Laughlin, Nancy Bartlett, 1
Lawrence, D.H., 117
LEARNING, 64
legends, 177
Leonardo da Vinci, 179
Leonardo's Head of Christ, 119, 124, 131
Leroi, Vera, 2
life as a totality, 134
life forces, 16, 105
life-force organism, 94
light, 117, 166, 173
limbs, 100, 118
limestone, 90, 102
Lindenberg, Christoph, 48
line, ideal straight, 145
line, straight or curved, 156

logical reasoning, 150
loneliness, 111
Lucifer, 83

M

machine, 36, 117
MacKaye (Ege), Arvia, 1
main lesson, 31
man and animal, 23, 88, 99
Mann, A.W., 129
manners, 151
maps, 170
materialism, 143, 168
mathematics, 108, 142, 149
Medieval art, 112
medieval romances, 139
Menes, King, 130
Mephisto, 50
metabolism, 153
metals, 91
metamorphosis, 135, 137, 161
metamorphosis-forms, 158
Michael Hall, 193
Michelangelo's Bound Slave, 129
Middle Ages, 141
mineralogy, 88
modelling, 79
Modern Art of Education, 15
Molière, 168
Molt, Emil, 5, 35
money, gift, 58
monomaniac thinking, 49
moral power, 198
morality, 98, 104, 169
Morning Verse, 66
motor and sense activity, 39
motor-sensory balance, 44
movement, 80
music, 111, 183, 189
musical abilities, 181

N

nature study, 88
naturalism, 164
naturalistic, 73
New York City, 88
Newton, 50, 116

Nietzsche, 169
Nile, 170
ninth grade, 81, 105, 107, 145, 187, 188
ninth and tenth grades, 166
Noll, Dr. Ludwig, 13
Norse legends, 177
North America, 193
noun, 185

O

observation, 81
Old Testament, 83, 130, 177
"open classrooms", 64
optics, 96

P

painting, 99
Pandora's box, 83
parents, 43, 54, 63, 106, 109, 126, 155, 193
Parsifal, 139
Parthenon, 173
Paulsen, Virginia, 2
Perceval, 141
perspective, 112, 164
Peterson, James, 59
Pharaoh, 129
phosphorus, 102
phrenologists, 119
physical body, 16, 74, 94, 154
physics, 73, 76, 88, 96, 108, 116
physiology, 107
picture, helpful, 102
picture of the child, 26
plant study, 69
play, 127
Plato, 17, 36, 143, 174
poetry, 110, 182
polarities, 111, 156
Poppelbaum, Dr. Hermann, 24
posture, 154
prayer, 16, 32, 154
pre-adolescence, 100
pre-school program, 57
principles, 24
projective geometry, 147

psychoanalysis, 26, 50, 136
psychology, 14, 18, 26, 37, 41, 49, 95, 133, 143, 166
puberty, 88
public schools, 59, 64
puppets, 94, 128
Pusch, Ruth, 3, 104
pyrite, 103

Q

quantum mechanics, 116
quarrels, 99, 137
quartz, 90
Querido, René, 181
quest, 140

R

radio, 43, 118
Radio Interview, 29
rationalism, 143
reductionism, 143
reincarnation, 17, 18
relativity theory, 116
Rembrandt, 113
Renaissance history, 106, 112
"Renewal", 221
responsibilities, 23
reverence, 33
rhythmical system, 16
ribbon-motifs, 161
romanticism, 188
Rome, 106, 112, 178
Romeo and Juliet, 107
rose window, 150
Rousseau, 40
Routledge, Shirley and Bob, 53
Rudolf Steiner School, New York, 1, 29, 126, 193
Rudolf Steiner schools, 28, 29
Russian, 181

S

sacrament, 151
Saint Francis, 135, 179
Saint John, 78
Sandkühler, Konrad, 192
Schiller, J. C. Friedrich, 168

schizophrenia, 137
schools, independent, 36
schools, public, 29, 59
Schweitzer, Albert, 175
science, 26, 32, 73, 76, 88, 97, 116, 118
scientists, 36
sculpture, 119, 174
second grade, 68, 101, 177, 183
self-education, 91
Sensitive Chaos, 85
sentient body, 106
service, 141
"seven year" periods, 94, 105, 126
seventh grade, 82, 100 -101, 105, 187
sex, 21, 133
Shakespeare, 168
sin, 109
Sir Gawain and the Green Knight, 140
sixth grade, 73, 76, 79, 88, 96, 101, 105, 163, 178, 185
skeleton, 120
Skinner, B. F., 37, 42
skull, 118
sleep, 16, 127, 161
Snow, Sir C. P., 36
snow, crystals, 85, 92, 150
social consciousness, 67
social creativity, 20
soul, 104, 143, 157
soul-being, 95
sound, 73
Spanish, 181
Spenser, 78
spiritual and cultural renewal, 55
spiritual evolution, 168
spiritual values, 32
Spock, Marjorie, 19
Staley, Betty, 87, 114
Starke, Georg, 94
statistics, 150
Stein, Dr. Walter Johannes, 13
Steiner, Marie, 13
Steiner, Rudolf, 7, 10, 34, 65, 66, 104, 111, 114, 154, 155

Stockmeyer, E.A. Carl, 11
stories, 183, 186
straight line, 145
student council, 151
Study of Man, 12, 64
Stuttgart, 11
sulfur, 101
surprise, 82
symmetry, 158

T

Table Prayer, 154
tabula rasa, 18
teacher, 22, 27, 30, 33, 98, 104, 106, 107
teachers, Waldorf, 10, 45, 57, 60, 75, 127, 132, 143, 158, 168, 180, 183, 192
teacher training, 197, 210, 213
teaching, 144, 149
teaching machines, 41
technical drawing, 81
technology, 37, 150
teeth, change of, 127
temperaments, 100, 127, 179, 180
temples, 172
Tennyson, 114
tenth grade, 81, 118, 166, 188
textbooks, 60, 185
theology, 143
thinking, 19, 64, 81, 98, 121, 133, 136, 157, 144, 190
thinking, linear, 48
third grade, 158, 177, 183
Thoreau, 40, 85
thought, 118, 119, 139, 153
threefold being, 14
Threefold Farm, 1
Threefold Social Order, 11
Tolstoy, 136
tool, 80
Toronto Waldorf School, 56
Tower of Babel, 83
Traherne, Thomas, 18
transformation of substance, 153
transformation, 135
transistor radios, 118
triangle, idea of a, 146

230

Tristan and Isolt, 140
TV watching, 43
twelfth grade, 123, 126, 189
twelve-year-olds, 88
two hour lesson, 31

V

vaccuum tubes, 117
van der Post, Laurens, 138
Vaughan, Henry, 18
verb, 185
"Vibrating World", 77
vibrations, 74
volcano, 90
von Baravalle, Hermann, 164, 196
Von Heydebrand, Caroline, 12

W

Wagner, Richard, 140
Wagner, Wolfgang, 79
Waldorf Astoria Cigarette Factory, 14
Waldorf School, first, 35, 193
Waldorf School of Garden City, 151, 193
Waldorf schools, 8, 38, 53, 210-218
Waller, Mary, 77
Waller, Mieta, 13
warmth, 154
water, 85, 117
Whitman, Walt, 196
whole human being, 25
wholeness, 68, 119, 134
wickedness, 94
will, 19, 64, 79, 81, 119, 122, 125, 164
Winckler, Dr. Franz, 134
wish, 82
wonder, 82, 84
wood carving, 81
woodwork, 79
work, 47
workshops, 65
writing, foreign language, 185

Y

Young, John W., 147

Z

zoology, 99

* * *

231

main

372.21 WALDORF

Waldorf schools, volume 2

PORTLAND PUBLIC LIBRARY
5 MONUMENT SQ.
PORTLAND, ME 04101

DATE DUE		
APR 17 2001		
NOV 17 2001		
JUL 1 8 2002	JUL 2 3 2005	
JUL 0 8 2003	JUL 1 6 2006	
SEP 2 9 2003	MAY 2 0 2009	
JUN 0 6 2005		